# THE HOURS OF TH
## OUR LORD JESUS CHRIST

**Luisa Piccarreta**
**The Little Daughter of the Divine Will**

Ad usum privatum
www.divinewill.eu

# Content

## Ecclesiastical seals of approval of the original Italian editions of this book

**First edition**

Revisione arcivescovile, Naples, February 20 , 1915

**Nihil Obstat**: Francesco Sorrentino (Revisore eccl.)

**Imprimatur**: A. Can. Laviano, V.G.

**Second edition**

Revisione arcivescovile, Naples, 1916

**Nihil obstat**: Francesco Sorrentino (Revisore eccl.)

**Imprimatur**: A. Can. Laviano, V.G.

**Third edition** Revisione arcivescovile, Naples, 1917

**Reimprimatur**: Francesco Sorrentino (Revisore eccl.)

**Fourth edition**

Messina, August 8, 1924

**Nihil Obstat**: D. Prestifillipo, SJ

**Fifth edition**

Taranto, Curia Archiepiscopale, August 28, 1934

**Nihil Obstat**: Delegato dall'Arcviesco, Giuseppe Blandamura

# Introductory note

St. Hannibal of Francia, Luisa's extraordinary confessor affirms that her method is a "totally new approach," and she was the first to introduce this way of contemplating the Lord's passion:

I was doing the Hours of the Passion and Jesus, all pleased, told me: "My daughter, if you knew what great satisfaction I feel in seeing you repeating these Hours of my Passion - always repeating them, over and over again - you would be happy. It is true that my Saints have meditated on my Passion and have comprehended how much I suffered, melting in tears of compassion, so much so, as to feel consumed for love of my pains; but not in such a continuous way, and repeated many times in this order. Therefore I can say that you are the first one to give Me this pleasure, so great and special, as you keep fragmenting within you - hour by hour - my life and what I suffered. And I feel so drawn that, hour by hour, I give you this food and I eat the same food with you, doing what you do together with you. Know, however, that I will reward you abundantly with new light and new graces; and even after your death, each time souls on earth will do these Hours of my Passion, in Heaven I will clothe you with ever new light and glory."[1]

---

[1] November 4, 1914

# Preface

## by Saint Annibale M. di Francia

Messina, October 29, 1926

Intelligentes quae sit voluntas Dei.

We begin, with this first printing, the publication of more than 20 handwritten volumes of sublime revelations which, always excepting the judgments of the Holy Church, we piously believe to have been given by Our Lord Jesus Christ to a soul, a dearest daughter and disciple of His, who is the pious author of the Hours of the Passion.

Even now we make known that these revelations, which are continuing and will continue, we don't know for how much longer, have as their goal the establishment of the complete Triumph of the Kingdom of the Divine Will upon earth.

(...) This solitary soul is a most pure virgin, wholly of God, who appears to be the object of singular predilection of Jesus, Divine Redeemer. It seems that Our Lord, who century after century increases the wonders of His Love more and more, wanted to make of this virgin with no education, whom He calls the littlest one that He found on earth, the instrument of a mission so sublime that no other can be compared to it - that is, the triumph of the Divine Will upon the whole earth, in conformity with what is said in the 'Our Father': Fiat Voluntas Tua sicut in Coelo et in terra.

## The Hours of the Passion

At the same time as the sublime revelations about the virtues in general, and about the Divine Will in particular, for many years, at nighttime, this soul has entered the contemplation of the sufferings of Our Lord Jesus Christ, with the addition of distinct information about many scenes of the Passion.

The method was that of going through the 24 hours of the Adorable Passion of Our Lord Jesus Christ, which begin with the Legal Supper and end with His death on the Cross. These visions were sometimes accompanied by corresponding revelations of Our Lord.

Since nothing was published of the visions and revelations of this soul, in her excessive desire to keep everything hidden, fearing that a publication, even anonymous, might uncover her, she wanted to bury this Treasure of divine knowledges, of superhuman compassion, of a superhuman fount of the most loving affections within herself.

But her Spiritual Father placed the majestic Lady Obedience, the strong Warrior armed from head to foot, before her; and Our Lord Himself pushed her to manifest them for the good of many souls.

She surrendered, and to the author of this Preface was entrusted the printing of the writings which she put on paper regarding this topic so important.

As the first Edition of this admirable Treatise of the 24 Hours of the Passion of Our Lord appeared, the blessing of God seemed evident. In a short time all copies were depleted, which at that time were 5,000, without being sent to specific addresses. It was enough to send one copy to some devout person, that requests would begin to arrive. An announcement was placed in the periodical of our Anthonian Orphanages "Dio e il Prossimo" ["God and Neighbor"] under the name of a Book of Gold, and immediately the requests increased, in such a way that the Edition was soon exhausted.

Most Eminent Cardinal Cassetta, to whom nothing had been sent directly, requested 50 copies at once.

Then came the 2nd Edition, a larger one, and then the 3rd. Both of them were rapidly depleted.

For the purpose of promotion, sales were made at moderate prices, just to cover the expenses.

At that time a pleasant circumstance occurred, which we remember with pleasure. A letter, addressed directly to me, arrived from the Vatican, written by that angelic Bishop - today Apostolic Nuncio of Venezuela, at that time the Secretary of Bishop Msgr. Tacci (who is today an emeritus Cardinal) - Msgr. Cento, who was then appointed Bishop of Acireale, and will perhaps be a Cardinal of the Holy Church. There had been no previous contacts between this lovable person and myself. In this letter he appeared enthusiastic from the reading of the Hours of the Passion by an "unknown author", and he prayed me to reveal to him her name and address, because he wanted to correspond with her about things of the spirit. (...)

# THE TWENTY-FOUR HOURS OF THE PASSION

## Preparation before each hour

O my Lord Jesus Christ, prostrate in your divine presence, I implore your most loving Heart to admit me to the sorrowful meditation of the 24 hours in which for love of us You wanted to suffer so much, in your adorable body and in your most holy soul, unto death on the Cross. O please, give me help, grace, love, deep compassion and understanding of your sufferings, as I now meditate the __ Hour.

And for those which I cannot meditate, I offer You my will to meditate them, and I willingly intend to meditate them in all the hours in which I have to apply myself to my duties, or sleep.

Accept, O merciful Lord, my loving intention, and let it be beneficial for me and for all, as if I effectively and in a saintly way accomplished what I wish to practice.

Meanwhile, I give You thanks, O my Jesus, for calling me to union with You by means of prayer. And to please You more, I take your thoughts, your tongue, your Heart, and with this I intend to pray, fusing all of myself in your Will and in your love; and stretching out my arms to hug You, I place my head on your Heart, and I begin.

## Thanksgiving after each hour

My lovable Jesus, You have called me in this hour of your Passion to keep You company, and I have come. I seemed to hear You praying, repairing and suffering, in anguish and sorrow, pleading for the salvation of souls in the most touching and eloquent voices.

I tried to follow You in everything; and now, having to leave You for my usual occupations, I feel the duty to say to You, 'Thank You' and 'I bless You.'

Yes, O Jesus, I repeat to You 'Thank You' thousands and thousands of times, and 'I bless You' for all that You have done and suffered for me and for all. I thank You and I bless You for every drop of Blood You shed, for every breath, for every heartbeat, for every step, word, glance, bitterness and offense which You endured. In everything, O my Jesus, I intend to seal You with a 'Thank You' and an 'I bless You.'

Please, O Jesus, let my whole being send You a continuous flow of thanks and blessings, so as to draw upon me and upon everyone the flow of your blessings and thanks. Please, O Jesus, press me to your Heart, and with your most holy hands seal every particle of my being with your 'I bless you', so that nothing other than a continuous hymn to You may come from me.

# First Hour

From 5 to 6 PM

## Jesus takes leave of His Most Holy Mother

O Celestial Mama, the hour of the separation is approaching, and I come to You. O Mother, give me your love and your reparations; give me your sorrow, because together with You I want to follow, step by step, adored Jesus.

And now Jesus comes to You, and You, with heart overflowing with love, run toward Him and in seeing Him so pale and sad, your Heart aches with pain, your strengths leave You and You are about to fall at His feet.

O my sweet Mama, do You know why adorable Jesus has come to You? Ah, He has come to say the last good-bye, to tell You the last word, to receive the last embrace!

O Mother, I cling to You with all the tenderness of which my poor heart is capable, so that clinging and bound to You, I too may receive the embraces of adored Jesus. Will You perhaps disdain me? Isn't it rather a comfort for your Heart to have a soul near You, who would share its pains, affections and reparations?

O Jesus, in such a harrowing hour for your most tender Heart, what a lesson of filial and loving obedience to your Mama You give us! What a sweet harmony passes between You and Mary! What a sweet enchantment of love rises up to the throne of the Eternal One and extends for the salvation of all creatures of the earth!

O my Celestial Mama, do You know what adored Jesus wants from You? Nothing but your last blessing. It is true that from every particle of your being nothing but blessings and praises come out for your Creator; but Jesus, in taking leave of You, wants to hear the sweet word: "I bless You, O Son". And that "I bless You" removes all the blasphemies from His hearing, and descends, sweet and gentle, into His Heart. Jesus wants your "I bless You", almost to place it as a shelter from all the offenses of creatures.

I too unite myself to You, O sweet Mama. Upon the wings of the winds I want to go around the heavens to ask the Father, the Holy Spirit and all the Angels, for an "I bless You" for Jesus, so that, as I go to Him, I may bring Him their blessings. And here on earth, I want to go to all creatures and ask, from every lip, from every heartbeat, from every step, from every breath, from every gaze, from every thought - blessings and praises for Jesus. And if no one wants to give them to me, I intend to give them for them.

O sweet Mama, after going round and round, to ask the Sacrosanct Trinity, the Angels, all creatures, the light of the sun, the fragrance of the flowers, the waves of the sea, every breath of wind, every spark of fire, every moving leaf, the twinkling of the stars, every movement of nature, for an "I bless You", I come to You and I place all my blessings together with yours.

My sweet Mama, I see that You receive comfort and relief, and that You offer Jesus all my blessings in reparation for the blasphemies and the maledictions which He receives from creatures. But as I offer You everything, I hear your trembling voice saying: "Son, bless me too!"

O my sweet Love, Jesus, bless me also, together with your Mama; bless my thoughts, my heart, my hands, my works, my steps, and with your Mother, all creatures.

O my Mother, in looking at the face of sorrowful Jesus, pale, sad, harrowing, the memory of the pains which He is about to suffer awakens in You. You foresee His face covered with spit and You bless it, His head pierced by the thorns, His eyes blinded, His body tortured by the scourges, His hands and feet pierced by the nails; and wherever He is about to go, You follow Him with your blessings. And I too will follow Him together with You. When Jesus is struck by the scourges, crowned with thorns, slapped, pierced by the nails, everywhere He will find my "I bless You" together with yours.

O Jesus, O Mother, I compassionate You. Immense is your pain in these last moments. The Heart of one seems to tear the Heart of the other.

O Mother, snatch my heart from the earth and bind it tightly to Jesus, so that, clinging to Him, I may share in His pains, and as You cling to each other, as You embrace, as You exchange the last glances, the last kisses, being in-between your two Hearts, may I receive your last kisses, your last embraces. Don't You see that I cannot be without You, in spite of my misery and my coldness?

Jesus, Mama, keep me close to You; give me your love, your Will. Dart through my poor heart, hold me tightly in your arms; and together with You, O sweet Mother, I want to follow, step by step, adored Jesus, with the intention of giving Him comfort, relief, love and reparation for all.


O Jesus, together with your Mama, I kiss your left foot, asking You to forgive me and all creatures, for all the times we have not walked toward God.

I kiss your right foot: forgive me and all for all the times we have not followed the perfection You wanted from us.

I kiss your left hand: communicate to us your purity.

I kiss your right hand: bless all of my heartbeats, thoughts, affections, so that, given value by your blessing, they all may be sanctified. And with me, bless all creatures, and seal the salvation of their souls with your blessing.

O Jesus, I embrace You together with your Mama, and kissing your Heart, I pray You to place my heart between your two Hearts, that it may be nourished continuously by your love, by your sorrows, by your very affections and desires, and by your own Life. Amen.


## REFLECTIONS AND PRACTICES
## by St. Hannibal di Francia


Before giving start to His Passion, Jesus goes to His Mother to ask for Her blessing. In this act Jesus teaches us obedience, not only external but also interior, which we must have in order to reciprocate the inspirations of grace. Sometimes we are not ready to put into practice a good inspiration, either because we are held back by love of self united to temptation, or because of human respect, or in order not to use holy violence on ourselves.

But rejecting the good inspiration of exercising a virtue, of accomplishing a virtuous act, of doing a good work, or of practicing a devotion, makes the Lord withdraw, depriving us of new inspirations.

On the other hand, the prompt correspondence, pious and prudent, to holy inspirations attracts more lights and graces upon us.

In the cases of doubt, one should turn promptly and with righteous intention to the great means of prayer and to upright and experienced advice. In this way, the good God will enlighten the soul to execute the healthy inspiration, increasing it for her greater benefit.

We must do our actions, our acts, our prayers, the Hours of the Passion, with the same intentions of Jesus, in His Will, sacrificing ourselves as He did, for the glory of the Father and for the good of souls.

We must place ourselves in the disposition of sacrificing ourselves in everything for love of our lovable Jesus, conforming to His spirit, operating with His own sentiments, and abandoning ourselves in Him, not only in all the external sufferings and adversities, but much more in all that He will dispose in our interior. In this way, at any time, we will find ourselves ready to accept any suffering. By doing this, we will give sweet sips to our Jesus. Then, if we do all this in the Will of God which contains all sweetnesses and all contentments in immense proportion, we will give to Jesus large sweet sips, so as to mitigate the poisoning which other creatures cause Him, and to console His Divine Heart.

Before starting any action, let us always invoke the blessing of God, so that our actions may have the touch of the Divinity, and may attract His blessings not only on us, but upon all creatures.

My Jesus, may your blessing precede me, accompany me and follow me, so that everything I do may carry the seal of your 'I bless you.'

# Second Hour

From 6 to 7 PM

## Jesus departs from His Most Holy Mother and sets out for the Cenacle

My adorable Jesus, as I have shared in your sufferings together with You, and in those of your afflicted Mama, I see that You are about to leave to go there, where the Will of the Father calls You. The love between Son and Mother is so great as to render You inseparable, so You leave Yourself in the Heart of your Mama, and the Queen and sweet Mama places Herself into yours; otherwise it would have been impossible for You to separate. But then, blessing each other, You give Her the last kiss to strengthen Her in the bitter pains She is about to suffer; and giving Her your last good-bye, You leave.

But the paleness of your face, your trembling lips, your suffocated voice, as though wanting to burst into tears in saying good-bye – ah, everything tells me how much You love Her and how much You suffer in leaving Her!

But to fulfill the Will of the Father, with your Hearts fused into each other, You submit Yourselves to everything, wanting to repair for those who, unwilling to overcome the tendernesses of relatives and friends, and bonds and attachments, do not care about fulfilling the Holy Will of God and corresponding to the state of sanctity to which God calls them. What sorrow do these souls not give You, in rejecting from their hearts the love You want to give them, contenting themselves with the love of creatures!

My lovable Love, as I repair with You, allow me to remain with your Mama in order to console Her and sustain Her, while You leave. Then I will hasten my steps to come and reach You. But to my greatest sorrow, I see that my anguishing Mama shivers, and Her pain is such that, as She tries to say good-bye to Her Son, Her voice dies on Her lips, and She is unable to utter a word. She is about to faint, and in Her swoon of love, She says: "My Son, my Son! I bless You! What a bitter separation – more cruel than any death!" But the pain yet prevents Her from uttering a word, and makes Her mute!

Disconsolate Queen, let me sustain You, dry your tears and compassionate You in your bitter sorrow! My Mama, I will not leave You alone; and You - take me with You and teach me, in these moments so painful for You and for Jesus, what I have to do, how to defend Him, repair Him and console Him, and whether I must lay down my life to defend His.

No, I will not move from under your mantle. At your wish, I will fly to Jesus; I will bring Him your love, your affections, your kisses together with mine, and I will place them in each wound, in every drop of His Blood, in every pain and insult, so that, in feeling the kisses and the love of His Mama in each pain, His sufferings may be sweetened. Then I will come again under your mantle, bringing You His kisses to sweeten your pierced Heart. My Mama, my heart is pounding, I want to go to Jesus. And as I kiss your maternal hands, bless me as You blessed Jesus, and allow me to go to Him.

My sweet Jesus, love directs me toward your steps and I reach You, as You walk along the streets of Jerusalem together with your beloved disciples. I look at You and I see You still pale. I hear your voice, sweet, yes, but sad - so much as to break the heart of your disciples, who feel troubled.

"This is the last time", You say, "that I walk along these streets by Myself. Tomorrow I will walk through them, bound and dragged among a thousand insults". And pointing out the places where You will be most insulted and tortured, You continue: "My life down here is about to set, just as the sun is now setting, and tomorrow at this hour I will no longer be here! But, like sun, I will rise again on the third day!"

At your words, the Apostles become sad and taciturn, not knowing what to answer. But You add: "Courage, do not lose heart; I will not leave you, I will be always with you. But it is necessary that I die for the good of you all."

In saying these words, You are moved, but with trembling voice You continue to instruct them. And before enclosing Yourself in the cenacle, You look at the sun which is setting, just as your life is setting; You offer your steps for those who find themselves at the setting of their lives, giving them the grace to let them set in You, and repairing for those who, in spite of the sorrows and disillusions of life, are obstinate in not wanting to surrender to You.

Then You look at Jerusalem again, the center of your prodigies and of the predilections of your Heart - Jerusalem which, in return, is preparing your cross and sharpening the nails to commit the deicide; and You tremble, your Heart breaks - and You cry over its destruction.

With this, You repair for many souls consecrated to You, whom You tried to form with so much care as portents of your love, but ungrateful and unrequiting, they make You suffer more bitternesses! I want to repair together with You, to sweeten the stabbing of your Heart.

But I see that You are horrified at the sight of Jerusalem, and withdrawing your gaze, You enter the cenacle. My Love, hold me tightly to your Heart, that I may make your bitternesses my own, to offer them together with You. And You, look with pity upon my soul, and pouring your love into it - bless me.

## REFLECTIONS AND PRACTICES
### by St. Hannibal di Francia

Jesus promptly departs from His Mother, although His most tender Heart undergoes a shock.

Are we ready to sacrifice even the most legitimate and holy affections in order to fulfill the Divine Volition?

(Let us examine ourselves especially in the cases of separation from the sense of the Divine Presence and from sensible devotion).

Jesus did not take His last steps in vain. In them, He glorified the Father and asked for the salvation of souls. We must place in our steps the same intentions which Jesus placed - that is, to sacrifice ourselves for the glory of the Father and for the good of souls. We must also imagine placing our steps in those of Jesus Christ; and as Jesus Christ did not take them in vain, but enclosed in His steps those of creatures, repairing for all their missteps, to give the glory due to the Father, and life to all the missteps of creatures so that they might walk along the

19

path of good - we should do it in the same way, placing our steps in those of Jesus Christ with His own intentions.

Do we walk on the street modest and composed, so as to be an example for others? As the afflicted Jesus walked, He talked to the Apostles every once in a while, speaking to them about His imminent Passion. What do we say in our conversations?

When the opportunity arises, do we make the Passion of the Divine Redeemer the object of our conversations?

In seeing the Apostles sad and discouraged, loving Jesus tried to comfort them. Do we place in our conversations the intention of relieving Jesus Christ? Do we try to do them in the Will of God, infusing in others the spirit of Jesus Christ? Jesus goes to the Cenacle. We must enclose our thoughts, affections, heartbeats, prayers, actions, food and work in the Heart of Jesus Christ in the act of operating. By doing this, our actions will acquire the divine attitude. However, since it is difficult to always keep this divine attitude, because it is hard for the soul to fuse her acts continuously in Him, the soul can compensate with the attitude of her good will. Jesus will be very pleased. He will become the vigilant sentry of each of her thoughts, words and heartbeats. He will place these acts as cortege inside and outside of Himself, watching them with great love, as the fruit of the good will of the creature. When then the soul, fusing herself in Him, does her immediate acts[1] with Jesus, good Jesus will feel so attracted toward that soul that He will do what she does together with her, turning the work of the creature into Divine work. All this is the effect of the Goodness of God which takes everything into account and rewards everything, even a tiny act in the Will of God, so that the creature may not be defrauded of anything.

O my Life and my All, may your steps direct mine, and as I tread the earth, let my thoughts be in Heaven!

## Third Hour

From 7 to 8 PM

## The Legal Supper

O Jesus, You now arrive at the cenacle together with your beloved disciples and You begin your supper with them. How much sweetness, how much affability You show through all your person, as You lower Yourself to taking material food for the last time! Everything is love in You; also in this, You not only repair for the sins of gluttony, but You impetrate the sanctification of food.

Jesus, my life, your sweet and penetrating gaze seems to search all of the Apostles; and also in this act of taking food your Heart remains pierced in seeing your dear Apostles still weak and listless, especially the perfidious Judas, who has already put a foot in hell. And You, from the bottom of your Heart, say bitterly: "What is the utility of my Blood? Here is a soul so favored by Me – yet, he is lost!"

And You look at him with your eyes refulgent with light and love, as though wanting to make him understand the great evil he is about to commit. But your supreme charity makes You bear this sorrow and You do not make it manifest even to your beloved disciples.

And while You grieve for Judas, your Heart is filled with joy in seeing, on your left, your beloved disciple John; so much so, that unable to contain your love any longer, drawing him sweetly to Yourself, You let him place his head upon your Heart, letting him experience paradise in advance.

It is in this solemn hour that the two peoples, the reprobate and the elect, are portrayed by the two disciples: the reprobate in Judas, who already feels hell in his heart; the elect in John, who rests and delights in You.

O my sweet Good, I too place myself near You, and together with your beloved disciple I want to place my weary head upon your adorable Heart, praying You to let me experience the delights of Heaven, also on this earth; so that, enraptured by the sweet harmonies of your Heart, the earth may no longer be earth for me, but Heaven.

But in the midst of those most sweet and divine harmonies, I hear sorrowful heartbeats escaping You: these are for lost souls! O Jesus, o please, do not allow any more souls to be lost. Let your heartbeat, flowing through them, make them feel the heartbeats of the life of Heaven, just as your beloved disciple John felt them; so that, attracted by the gentleness and sweetness of your love, they may all surrender to You.

O Jesus, as I remain upon your Heart, give food also to me, as You gave it to the Apostles: the food of love, the food of the divine word, the food of your Divine Will. O my Jesus, do not deny me this food, which You so much desire to give me so that your very Life may be formed in me.

My sweet Good, while I remain close to You, I see that the food You are taking together with your dear disciples is nothing but a lamb. This is a figurative lamb: just as this lamb has no vital humor left by force of fire, so You, mystical Lamb, having to consume Yourself completely for creatures by force of love, will keep not even a drop of blood for Yourself, but will pour it all out for love of us.

O Jesus, there is nothing You do which does not portray vividly your most sorrowful Passion, which You keep always present in your mind, in your Heart - in everything. And this teaches me that if I too had the thought of your Passion before my mind and in my heart, You would never deny me the food of your love. How much I thank You!

O my Jesus, not one act escapes You which does not keep me present and which does not intend to do me a special good. So I pray You that your Passion be always in my mind, in my heart, in my gazes, in my steps and in my pains, so that, wherever I turn, inside and outside of myself, I may always find You present in me. And You, give me the grace never to forget what You have borne and suffered for me. May this be the magnet which, drawing my whole being into You, will never again allow me to go far away from You.

## REFLECTIONS AND PRACTICES
### by St. Hannibal di Francia

Before taking food, let us unite our intentions to those of our lovable and good Jesus, imagining having the mouth of Jesus in our mouths, and moving our tongues and cheeks together with His. By doing this, we will not only draw the life of Jesus Christ into ourselves, but we will unite to Him in order to give to the Father complete glory, praise, love, thanksgiving and reparation owed by creatures, which Jesus Himself offered in the act of taking food. Let us also imagine being at the table near Jesus Christ, now looking at Him, now praying Him to share a bite with us, now kissing the hem of His mantle, now contemplating the movements of His lips and of His celestial eyes, now noticing the sudden clouding of His most lovable Face in foreseeing so much human ingratitude!

Just as loving Jesus spoke about His Passion during supper, as we take our food, we will make some reflections on how we meditated the Hours of the Passion. The Angels hang on our words, to gather our prayers, our reparations, and take them before the Father in order to somehow mitigate the just indignation for the so many offenses received from creatures - just as they carried them when Jesus was on earth. And when we pray, can we say that the Angels were pleased; that we have been recollected and reverent, in such a way that they were able to joyously carry our prayers to Heaven, just as they carried those of our Jesus? Or did they rather remain saddened?

While afflicted Jesus was taking food, He remained transfixed at the sight of the loss of Judas; and in Judas He saw all the souls who were going to be lost. Since the loss of souls is the greatest of His pains, unable to contain it, He drew John to Himself in order to find relief. In the same way, we will remain always close to Him like John, compassionating Him in His pains, relieving Him, and giving Him rest in our hearts. We will make His pain our own, we will identify ourselves with Him, to feel the heartbeats of that Divine Heart, pierced by the loss of souls. We will give Him our own heartbeats in order to remove those wounds; and in the place of those wounds we will put the souls who want to be lost, so that they may convert and be saved.

Every beat of the Heart of Jesus is one 'I love you' which resounds in all the heartbeats of creatures, wanting to enclose all of them in His Heart in order to receive their heartbeats in return. But loving Jesus does not receive it from many, and therefore His heartbeat remains as though suffocated and embittered. Let us pray Jesus to seal our heartbeat with His 'I love you', so that our hearts too may live the life of His Heart and, resounding in the heartbeats of creatures, may force them to say, 'I love You, Jesus!' Even more, we will fuse ourselves in Him, and loving Jesus will let us hear His 'I love you' which fills Heaven and earth, circulates through the Saints, and descends into Purgatory. All the hearts of creatures are touched by this 'I love you'; even the elements feel new life, and all feel its effects. In His breathing too, Jesus feels as though suffocating for the loss of souls. And we will give Him our breath of love for His relief; and, taking His breath, we will touch the souls who detach themselves from His arms in order to give them the life of the divine breath, so that, instead of running away, they may return to Him, and cling more tightly to Him.

When we are in pain and almost feel that our breath cannot come out freely, let us think of Jesus, who contains the breath of creatures in His own breath. He too, as souls become lost, feels His breath being taken away. So, let us place our sorrowful and labored breath in the breath of Jesus in order to relieve Him; and let us run after the sinner with our pain, so as to force him to enclose himself in the Heart of Jesus.

My beloved Good, may my breath be a continuous cry at every creature's breath, forcing her to enclose herself in your breath.

The first word which loving Jesus pronounced on the Cross was a word of forgiveness, to justify all souls before the Father, and turn justice into mercy. We will give Him our acts to excuse the sinner, so that, moved by our apologies, He may not allow any soul to go to hell. We will unite with Him as sentries of the hearts of creatures, so that nobody may offend Him. We will let Him pour out His love, willingly accepting all that He may dispose for us - coldness, hardness, darkness, oppressions, temptations, distractions, slanders, illnesses and other things, so as to relieve Him from all that He receives from creatures. It is not by love alone that Jesus pours Himself out to souls. Many times, when He feels the coldness of other creatures, He goes to the soul and makes her feel His cold, to release Himself through her. If the soul accepts it, He will feel relieved from all the coldness of creatures, and this cold will be the sentry to someone else's heart, to make loving Jesus loved.

Other times, Jesus feels the hardness of hearts in His own, and unable to contain it, He wants to pour Himself out, and comes to us. He touches our hearts with His Heart, making us share in His pain. Making His pain our own, we will place it around the heart of the sinner in order to melt his hardness, and take him back to Him.

My beloved Good, You suffer greatly because of the loss of souls; and out of compassion I place my being at your disposal. I will take your pains and the pains of the sinners upon myself, leaving You relieved, and the sinner clinging to You.

O my Jesus, please, let my whole being be melted in love, so that I may be of continuous relief, to soothe all your bitternesses.

# Fourth Hour

From 8 to 9 PM

## The Eucharistic Supper

My sweet Love, always insatiable in your love, I see that as You finish the legal supper together with your dear disciples, You stand up, and united with them, You raise the hymn of thanksgiving to the Father for having given you food, wanting to repair for all the lack of thanksgiving of creatures, and for all the means He gives us for the preservation of corporal life. This is why, O Jesus, in anything You do, touch or see, You always have on your lips the words, "Thanks be to You, O Father". I too, Jesus, united with You, take the words from your very lips, and I will say, always and in everything: "Thank You for myself and for all", in order to continue the reparations for the lack of thanksgiving.

## The washing of the feet

But, O my Jesus, it seems that your love has no respite. I see that You make your beloved disciples sit down again; You take a bucket of water, wrap a white cloth around your waist and prostrate Yourself at the Apostles' feet, with a gesture so humble as to draw the attention of all Heaven, and to make It remain ecstatic. The Apostles themselves stay almost motionless in seeing You prostrate at their feet. But tell me, my Love, what do You want? What do You intend to do with this act so humble? Humility never before seen, and which will never be seen!

"Ah, my child, I want all souls, and prostrate at their feet like a poor beggar, I ask for them, I importune them and, crying, I plot love traps around them in order to obtain them!

Prostrate at their feet, with this bucket of water mixed with my tears, I want to wash them of any imperfection and prepare them to receive Me in the Sacrament.

I so much cherish this act of receiving Me in the Eucharist, that I do not want to entrust this office to the angels, and not even to my dear Mama, but I Myself want to purify them, down to the most intimate fibers, in order to dispose them to receive the fruit of the Sacrament; and in the Apostles I intended to prepare all souls.

I intend to repair for all the holy works and for the administration of Sacraments, especially those made by priests with a spirit of pride, empty of divine spirit and of disinterest. Ah, how many good works reach Me more to dishonor Me than to honor Me! More to embitter Me than to please Me! More to give Me death than to give Me life! These are the offenses which sadden Me the most. Ah, yes, my child, count all the most intimate offenses which they give Me, and repair with my own reparations. Console my embittered Heart."

O my afflicted Good, I make your life my own, and together with You I intend to repair for all these offenses. I want to enter into the most intimate hiding places of your Divine Heart and repair with your own Heart for the most intimate and secret offenses, which You receive from your dearest ones. O my Jesus, I want to follow You in everything, and together with You I want to go through all the souls who are about to receive You in the Eucharist, enter into their hearts, and place my hands together with yours, to purify them.

O please, O Jesus, with these tears of yours and this water with which You washed the feet of the Apostles, let us wash the souls who must receive You; let us purify their hearts; let us inflame them, and shake off the dust with which they are dirtied, so that, when they receive You, You may find in them your satisfactions, instead of your bitternesses.

But, my affectionate Good, while You are all intent on washing the feet of the Apostles, I look at You, and I see another sorrow which pierces your Most Holy Heart. These Apostles represent all the future children of the Church, and each of them, the series of each one of your sorrows. In some, weaknesses, in some, deceits; in one, hypocrisies, in the other, excessive love for interests; in Saint Peter the lack of firmness and all the offenses of the leaders of the Church; in Saint John the offenses of your most faithful ones; in Judas all of the apostates, with all the series of great evils which they commit.

Ah, your sorrow is suffocated by pain and by love; so much so, that unable to contain it, You pause at the feet of each Apostle and burst into tears, praying and repairing for each one of these offenses, and impetrating the appropriate remedy for all.

My Jesus, I too unite myself to You; I make your prayers, your reparations and your appropriate remedies for each soul, my own. I want to mix my tears with yours, that You may never be alone, but may always have me with You, to share in your pains.

But, sweet Love of mine, as You continue to wash the feet of the Apostles, I see that You are now at Judas' feet. I hear your labored breath. I see that You not only cry, but sob, and as You wash those feet, You kiss them, You press them to your Heart; and unable to speak with your voice because it is suffocated by crying, You look at him with eyes swollen with tears, and say to him with your Heart: "My child, O please, I beg you with the voices of my tears - do not go to hell! Give Me your soul, which I ask of you, prostrate at your feet. Tell Me, what do you want? What do you demand? I will give you everything, provided that you do not lose yourself. O please, spare this sorrow to Me, your God!" And again, You press those feet to your Heart. But in seeing the hardness of Judas, your Heart is cornered; your Heart suffocates You, and You are about to faint. My Heart and my Life, allow me to sustain You in my arms. I understand that these are your loving stratagems, which You use with each obstinate sinner.

O please, I pray You, my Heart - as I compassionate You and repair for the offenses which You receive from the souls who are obstinate in not wanting to convert, let us go around the earth, and wherever there are obstinate sinners, let us give them your tears to soften them, your kisses and your squeezes of love to bind them to You, in such a way that they will not be able to escape, and will therefore relieve You from the pain of the loss of Judas.

## Institution of the Eucharist

My Jesus, my joy and delight, I see that your love runs, and runs rapidly. You stand up, sorrowful as You are, and You almost run to the altar where there is bread and wine ready for the Consecration. I see You, my Heart, assuming a look wholly new and never seen before: your Divine Person acquires a tender, loving, affectionate appearance; your eyes blaze with light, more than if they were suns; your rosy face is radiant; your lips are smiling and burning with love; your creative hands assume the attitude of creating. I see You, my Love, all transformed: your Divinity seems to overflow from your Humanity.

My Heart and my Life, Jesus, this appearance of yours, never before seen, draws the attention of all the Apostles. They are caught by a sweet enchantment and do not dare even to breathe. Your sweet Mama runs in spirit to the foot of the altar, to admire the portents of your love. The Angels descend from Heaven, asking themselves: "What is this? What is this? These are true follies, true excesses! A God who creates, not heaven or earth, but Himself. And where? In the most wretched matter of a little bread and a little wine."

But while they are all around You, Oh insatiable Love, I see that You take the bread in your hands; You offer it to the Father, and I hear your most sweet voice say: "Holy Father, thanks be to You, for always answering your Son. Holy Father, concur with Me. One day, You sent Me from Heaven to earth to be incarnated in the womb of my Mama, to come and save Our children. Now, allow Me to be incarnated in each Host, to continue their salvation and be life of each one of my children. Do You see, O Father? Few hours of my life are left: who would have the heart to leave my children orphaned and alone? Many are their enemies - the obscurities, the passions, the weaknesses to which they are subject. Who will help them? O please, I supplicate You to let Me stay in each Host, to be life of each one, and therefore put to flight their enemies; to be their light, strength and help in everything. Otherwise, where shall they go? Who will help them? Our works are eternal, my love is irresistible – I cannot leave my children, nor do I want to."

The Father is moved at the tender and affectionate voice of the Son. He descends from Heaven; He is already on the altar, and united with the Holy Spirit, concurs with the Son. And Jesus, with sonorous and moving voice, pronounces the words of the Consecration, and without leaving Himself, creates Himself in that bread and wine.

Then You communicate your Apostles, and I believe that our celestial Mama did not remain without receiving You. Ah, Jesus, the heavens bow down and all send to You an act of adoration in your new state of profound annihilation.

But, O sweet Jesus, while your love remains pleased and satisfied, having nothing left to do, I see,

O my Good, on this altar, Hosts which will perpetuate until the end of centuries; and lined up in each Host, your whole sorrowful Passion, because the creatures, at the excesses of your love, prepare for You excesses of ingratitude and enormous crimes. And I, Heart of my heart, want to be always with You in each Tabernacle, in all the pyxes and in each consecrated Host which will ever be until the end of the world, to emit my acts of reparation, according to the offenses You receive.

O Jesus, I contemplate You in the Holy Host, and as though seeing You in your adorable Person, I kiss your majestic forehead; but in kissing You, I feel the pricks of your thorns. O my Jesus, in this Holy Host, how many creatures do not spare You thorns. They come before You, and instead of sending You the homage of their good thoughts, they send You their evil thoughts; and You lower your head again as You did in the Passion, receiving and bearing the thorns of these evil thoughts. Oh my Love, I draw near You to share in your pains; I place all my thoughts in your mind in order to expel these thorns which sadden You so much. May each one of my thoughts flow in each one of your thoughts, to make an act of reparation for each evil thought, and therefore console your sad mind.

Jesus, my Good, I kiss your beautiful eyes; I see your loving gaze toward those who come before your presence, anxious to receive the return of their gazes of love. But how many come before You, and instead of looking at You and searching for You, look at things which distract them, and so deprive You of the pleasure You feel in the exchange of gazes of love! You cry, and as I kiss You, I feel my lips wet with your tears. My Jesus, do not cry; I want to place my eyes in yours to share in these pains with You, and to cry with You. And wanting to repair for all the distracted gazes of creatures, I offer You my gazes, always fixed in You.

Jesus, my Love, I kiss your most holy ears; I now see You intent on listening to what the creatures want from You, in order to console them. But, instead, they send to your ears prayers badly said, full of diffidence, prayers done out of habit; and in this Holy Host, your hearing is molested more than in your very Passion. O my Jesus, I want to take all the harmonies of Heaven and place them in your ears to repair You, and I want to place my ears in yours, not only to share these pains with You, but to offer You my continuous act of reparation, and to console You.

Jesus, my Life, I kiss your most holy Face; I see it bleeding, bruised and swollen. The creatures, O Jesus, come before the Holy Host, and with their indecent postures and evil discourses, instead of giving You honor, seem to send You slaps and spittle. And You, just like in the Passion, receive them in all peace and patience, and You bear everything! O Jesus, I want to place my face close to yours, not only to kiss You and to receive the insults which come to You from your creatures, but to share with You all your pains. With my hands, I intend to caress You, wipe off the spit, and press You tightly to my heart; and of my being, to make many tiny little pieces, placing them before You, like many souls who adore You; and to turn my movements into continuous prostrations, to repair for the dishonors You receive from all creatures.

My Jesus, I kiss your most holy lips; I see that in descending sacramentally into the hearts of your creatures, You are forced to lean on many cutting, impure, evil tongues. Oh, how embittered You remain! You feel as though poisoned by these tongues, and it is even worse when You descend into their hearts! O Jesus, if it were possible, I would want to be in the mouth of each creature, to turn into praises all the offenses You receive from them!

My weary Good, I kiss your most holy head. I see it tired, exhausted, and all occupied in your crafting of love. Tell me, what do You do? And You: "My child, in this Host I work from morning to evening, forming chains of love; and as souls come to Me, I bind them to my Heart. But do you know what they do to Me? Many wriggle free by force, shattering my loving chains; and since these chains are linked to my Heart, I am tortured and become delirious. Then, in breaking my chains, they render my crafting useless, looking for the chains of creatures. And they do this even in my presence, using Me in order to reach their own ends. This grieves Me so much as to make Me faint and rave."

How much compassion I feel for You, O Jesus! Your love is cornered, and in order to relieve you from the offenses You receive from these souls, I ask You to chain my heart with those chains broken by them, in order to give You my return of love in their place.

My Jesus, my Divine Archer, I kiss your breast. The fire You contain in it is such that, in order to give a little vent to your flames and to take a little break from your work, You begin to play with the souls who come to You, shooting arrows of love which come out from your breast toward them. Your game is to form arrows, darts, spears; and when they strike souls, You become festive. But many, O Jesus, reject them, sending You arrows of coldness, darts of lukewarmness, and spears of ingratitude in return. And You remain so afflicted as to cry bitterly! Oh Jesus, here is my breast, ready to receive not only your arrows destined to me, but also those which the other souls reject; so You will no longer remain defeated in your love game. In this way, I will also repair for the coldness, the lukewarmness and the ingratitude, which You receive from them.


Oh Jesus, I kiss your left hand, and I intend to repair for all the illicit or blameworthy touches, done in your presence; and I pray You always to hold me tightly to your Heart!


Oh Jesus, I kiss your right hand, and I intend to repair for all the sacrileges, especially the Masses badly celebrated! How many times, my Love, You are forced to descend from Heaven into unworthy hands and breasts; and even though You feel nausea for being in those hands, Love forces You to stay. Even more, in some of your ministers, You find the ones who renew your Passion, because, with their enormous crimes and sacrileges, they renew the Deicide! Jesus, I am frightened at this thought! But, alas, just as in the Passion You were in the hands of the Jews, You are in those unworthy hands, like a meek lamb, waiting, again, for your death and also for their conversion. Oh Jesus, how much You suffer! You would like a loving hand to free You from those bloodthirsty hands. O Jesus, when You are in those hands, I pray You to call me near You, and in order to repair You, I will cover You with the purity of the Angels, I will perfume You with your virtues to reduce the nausea You feel in being in those hands, and I will offer You my heart as escape and refuge. While You are in me, I will pray for priests, that they may be your worthy Ministers. Amen.

O Jesus, I kiss your left foot, and I intend to repair for those who receive You out of habit and without the necessary dispositions.

O Jesus, I kiss your right foot, and I intend to repair for those who receive You to offend You. O please, when they dare to do this, I pray You to renew the miracle You made to Longinus. Just as

You healed him and converted him at the touch of the Blood which gushed forth from your Heart, pierced by his lance, in the same way, at your sacramental touch, convert the offenses into love, and the offenders into lovers!

Oh Jesus, I kiss your most sweet Heart, into which all offenses pour, and I intend to repair for everything, to give You return of love for all, and to share in your pains, always together with You!

O Celestial Archer, if any offense escapes my reparation, I pray You to imprison me in your Heart and in your Will, so that I may repair for everything. I will pray the sweet Mama to keep me always with Her, in order to repair everything, and for everyone. We will kiss You together, and keeping You sheltered, we will drive away from You the waves of bitterness which You receive from creatures. O please, O Jesus, remember that I too am a poor sinful soul. Enclose me in your Heart, and with the chains of your love, do not only imprison me, but bind, one by one, my thoughts, my affections, my desires. Chain my hands and my feet to your Heart, that I may have no other hands and feet but Yours!

And so, my Love, my prison will be your Heart, my chains will be made of love; your flames will be my food, your breath will be mine, the fences preventing me from going out will be your Most Holy Will. So I will see nothing but flames, I will touch nothing but fire; and while they give me life, they will give me death, like that You suffer in the Holy Host. I will give You my life, and so, while I remain imprisoned in You, You will be released in me. Is this not your intent in imprisoning Yourself in the Host, in order to be released by the souls who receive You, becoming alive in them? And now, as a sign of love, bless me, give the mystical kiss of love to my soul, while I remain clasped and clinging to You.

O my sweet Heart, I see that after You have instituted the Most Holy Sacrament and have seen the enormous ingratitude and the offenses of creatures at the excesses of your love, although wounded and embittered, You do not draw back; rather, You want to drown everything in the immensity of your love.

I see You, O Jesus, as You administer Yourself to your Apostles, and then You add that they too must do what You have done, giving them authority to consecrate; so You ordain them priests and institute the other Sacraments. You take care of everything, and You repair for everything: the sermons badly given, the Sacraments administered and received without disposition, and therefore without effects; the mistaken vocations of priests, on their part and on the part of those who ordain them, not using all means in order to discern the true vocations. Ah, nothing escapes You, O Jesus, and I intend to follow You and to repair for all these offenses.

Then, after You have given fulfillment to everything, You gather your Apostles and set out for the Garden of Gethsemani, to begin your sorrowful Passion. I will follow You in everything, to keep You faithful company.

## REFLECTIONS AND PRACTICES
## by St. Hannibal di Francia

Jesus is hidden in the Host to give life to all. In His hiddenness, He embraces all centuries and gives light to all. In the same way, hiding ourselves in Him, we will give life and light to all with our prayers and reparations, even to the heretics and to the unfaithful, because Jesus does not exclude anyone.

What should we do in our hiddenness? In order to become similar to Jesus Christ, we must hide everything in Him: thoughts, glances, words, heartbeats, affections, desires, steps and works; even our prayers - we should hide them in the prayers of Jesus. And just as loving Jesus embraces all centuries in the Eucharist, we will also embrace them. Clinging to Him, we will be the thought of every mind, the word of every tongue, desire of every heart, step of every foot, work of every arm. By doing this, we will divert from the Heart of Jesus all the evils which all creatures would do to Him, trying to substitute for this

40

evil with all the good we can do, and pressing Jesus to give salvation, sanctity and love to all souls.

In order to reciprocate the life of Jesus, our life must be fully conformed to His own. The soul must have the intention of being in all the Tabernacles of the world in order to continuously keep Him company, and to give Him continuous relief and reparation; and with this intention do all the actions of the day. The first tabernacle is within us, in our heart; therefore we must pay great attention to all that good Jesus wants to do in us. Many times, being in our heart, Jesus makes us feel the need of prayer. Ah, it is Jesus that wants to pray, and wants us together with Him, almost identifying Himself with our voice, with our affection and with all our heart in order to make our prayer be one with His own! So, in order to give honor to the prayer of Jesus, we will be attentive to give Him all our being, so that loving Jesus may raise His prayer to speak to the Father, and renew in the world the effects of His own prayer.

We need to pay attention to each one of our interior motions, because good Jesus now makes us suffer, now wants us in prayer, now places us in one interior state, now in another, in order to repeat His own life in us.

Let us suppose that Jesus places us in the circumstance of exercising patience. He receives such grave and so many offenses from creatures, that He feels moved to resort to chastisements to strike the creatures. And here He gives us the opportunity to exercise patience. We must give Him honor, bearing everything with peace, just as Jesus does. Our patience will snatch from His hands the chastisements which other creatures draw from Him, because He will exercise His own Divine Patience within us. The same with all the other virtues, just as with patience. In the Sacrament, loving Jesus exercises all virtues; from Him we will draw fortitude, docility, patience, tolerance, humility, obedience.

Good Jesus gives us His flesh for food, and we will give Him our love, will, desires, thoughts and affections for His nourishment. In this way, we will compete with the love of Jesus. We will let nothing enter into us which is not Him; therefore, everything we will do - everything must serve to nourish our beloved Jesus. Our thought must feed the divine thought - that is, thinking that Jesus is hidden in us, and wants the nourishment of our thought. So, by thinking in a saintly way, we nourish the divine thought. Our words, heartbeats, affections, desires, steps, works - everything must serve to nourish Jesus. We must place the intention of feeding the creatures in Jesus.

O my sweet Love, in this hour You transubstantiated Yourself into bread and wine. Please, O Jesus, let all that I say and do be a continuous consecration of Yourself in me and in souls.

Sweet Life of mine, when You come into me, let my every heartbeat, desire, affection, thought and word feel the power of the sacramental consecration, so that, being consecrated, all my little being may become as many hosts in order to give You to souls.

O Jesus, sweet Love of mine, may I be your little host in order to enclose all of Yourself in me, like a living Host.

## Fifth Hour

From 9 to 10 PM

## First Hour of Agony in the Garden of Gethsemani

My afflicted Jesus, I feel drawn to this Garden as by an electric current. I comprehend that You, powerful magnet of my wounded heart, are calling me; and I run, thinking to myself: 'What are these attractions of love that I feel within me? Ah, maybe my persecuted Jesus is in such a state of bitterness as to feel the need of my company.' And I fly.

But – no! I feel horrified upon entering this Garden. The darkness of the night, the intensity of the cold, the slow moving of the leaves which, like feeble voices, announce pains, sadness and death for my sorrowful Jesus; the sweet glittering of the stars which, like crying eyes, are all intent on looking, reproach me for my ingratitude. And I tremble; gropingly, I go in search of Him, and I call Him: 'Jesus, where are You? You call me, and You do not show Yourself? You call me, and You hide?'

Everything is terror, everything is fright and profound silence. But I prick up my ears: I hear a labored breath, and it is Jesus Himself that I find. But what a dismal change! No longer is He the sweet Jesus of the Eucharistic Supper, whose face shone with radiant and enrapturing beauty; but He is sad, of a mortal sadness, such as to disfigure His native beauty. He already agonizes, and I feel

43

troubled in thinking that maybe I will no longer hear His voice, because He seems to be dying. So I cling to His feet; I become more brave – I draw near His arms and I place my hand on His forehead in order to sustain Him, and softly, I call Him: 'Jesus, Jesus!'

And He, stirred by my voice, looks at me and says: "Child, are you here? I was waiting for you. This was the sadness which oppressed Me the most: the total abandonment of all. And I was waiting for you, to let you be the spectator of my pains, and to let you drink, together with Me, the chalice of bitternesses which, in a little while, my Celestial Father will send Me through the Angel. We will sip from it together, because it will not be a chalice of comfort, but of intense bitternesses, and I feel the need of a few loving souls who would drink at least a few drops of it. This is why I called you

– that you may accept it, share with Me the pains, and assure Me that you will not leave Me alone in such great abandonment."

'Ah, yes my panting Jesus, we will drink together the chalice of your bitternesses; we will suffer your pains, and I will never move from your side!'

And afflicted Jesus, assured by me, enters into mortal agony, and suffers pains never before seen or understood. And I, unable to resist and wanting to compassionate Him and relieve Him, say to Him: 'Tell me, why are You so sad, afflicted and alone in this Garden and in this night? This is the last night of your life on earth; a few hours are left for You to begin your Passion. I thought I would find at least the Celestial Mama, the loving Magdalene, the faithful Apostles; but instead, I find You all alone, prey to a sadness which gives You a ruthless death, without making You die. Oh my Good and my All, You do not answer me? Speak to me!' But it seems You have no speech, so much is the sadness which oppresses You. But, oh my Jesus, that gaze of yours, full of light, yes, but afflicted and searching, such that it seems to be looking for help; your pale face, your lips parched with love, your Divine Person, trembling from head to foot, your heart, beating so intensely – and those heartbeats search for souls and cause You such labor that it seems that, any moment now, You are about to breathe your last – everything tells me that You are alone, and therefore You want my company.

Here I am, O Jesus, together with You. But I don't have the heart to see You cast on the ground. I take You in my arms, I press You to my heart; I want to count, one by one, your strainings, and, one by one, the offenses which advance toward You, in order to give You relief for everything, reparation for everything, and to give You at least one act of my compassion, for everything.

But, O my Jesus, while I hold You in my arms, your sufferings increase. My Life, I feel fire flowing in your veins, and I feel your Blood boiling, wanting to burst the veins to come out. Tell me, my Love, what is it? I do not see scourges, nor thorns, nor nails, nor cross; yet, as I place my head upon your Heart, I feel that cruel thorns pierce your head, that ruthless scourges spare not even one smallest part, inside and outside of your Divine Person, and that your hands are paralyzed and contorted, more than by nails. Tell me, my sweet Good, who has so much power, also in your interior, as to torment You and make You suffer as many deaths for as many torments as he gives You?

Ah, it seems that blessed Jesus opens His lips, faint and dying, and says to me: "My child, do you want to know what it is that torments Me more than the very executioners? Rather, those are nothing compared to this! It is the Eternal Love, which, wanting primacy in everything, is making Me suffer, all at once and in the most intimate parts, what the executioners will make Me suffer little by little. Ah, my child, it is Love which prevails in everything, over Me and within Me. Love is nail for Me, Love is scourge, Love is crown of thorns – Love is everything for Me. Love is my perennial passion, while that of men is in time. Ah, my child, enter into my Heart, come to be dissolved in my love, and only in my love will you comprehend how much I suffered and how much I loved you, and you will learn to love Me and to suffer only out of love."

O my Jesus, since You call me into your Heart to show me what love made You suffer, I enter into It. But as I enter, I see the portents of love, which crowns your head, not with material thorns, but with thorns of fire; which scourges You, not with lashes of ropes, but with lashes of fire; which crucifies You with nails, not made of iron, but of fire. Everything is fire, which penetrates deep into your bones and into your very marrow; and distilling all of your Most Holy Humanity into fire, it gives You mortal pains, certainly greater than the very Passion, and prepares a bath of love for all the souls who will want to be washed of any stain and acquire the right of children of love.

Oh, Love without end, I feel like drawing back before such immensity of love, and I see that in order to enter into love and to comprehend it, I should be all love! O my Jesus, I am not so! But since You want my company, and You want me to enter into You, I pray You to make me become all love.

And so I supplicate You to crown my head and each one of my thoughts with the crown of love. I implore You, O Jesus, to scourge my soul, my body, my powers, my feelings, my desires, my affections – in sum, everything, with the scourge of love; so that, in everything, I may be scourged and sealed by love. Oh endless Love, let there be nothing in me which does not take life from love.

O Jesus, center of all loves, I beg You to nail my hands and my feet, with the nails of love, so that, completely nailed by love - love I may become, love I may comprehend, with love I may be clothed, with love I may be nourished, and love may keep me completely nailed within You, so that nothing, inside and outside of me, may dare to divert me and take me away from Love, O Jesus!

## REFLECTIONS AND PRACTICES
## by St. Hannibal di Francia

In this hour, abandoned by His Eternal Father, Jesus Christ suffered such a burning fire of love as to be able to destroy all possible and imaginable sins, and to enflame with His love all creatures, even from millions and millions of worlds, and the lost souls of hell if they were not eternally obstinate in their evil. Let us enter into

Jesus, and after we have penetrated into His whole interior, in His most intimate fibers, in those heartbeats of fire, in His intelligence which was as though enflamed, let us take this love and clothe ourselves inside and out with the fire that burned Jesus. Then, coming out of Him and pouring ourselves into His Will, we will find there all creatures. Let us give the love of Jesus to each one of them, and touching their hearts and minds with this love let us try to transform them completely into love. Then, with the desires, with the heartbeats, with the thoughts of Jesus, let us form Jesus in every creature's heart. And then we will bring to Him all creatures who have Jesus in their hearts, and we will place them around Him, saying: 'O Jesus, we bring You all creatures with as many Jesuses in their hearts to give You relief and comfort. We have no other way to give relief to your love other than to bring every creature into your Heart!' By doing this, we will give true relief to Jesus, since the flames that burn Him are such that He keeps repeating: 'I burn, and there is nobody who takes my love. O please, give Me relief, take my love and give Me love!'

In order to conform to Jesus in everything, we must go back into ourselves, applying these reflections to ourselves: in all that we do, can we say that there is a continuous flow of love running between us and God? Our life is a continuous flow of love which we receive from God; if we think, there is a flow of love; if we work, there is a flow of love. The word is love, the heartbeat is love; we receive everything from God. But do all these actions run toward God with love? Does Jesus find in us the sweet enchantment of His love running toward Him, so that, enraptured by this enchantment, He may overflow with us with more abundant love?

If we have not placed the intention of running together in the love of Jesus in all that we have done, we will enter into ourselves and ask Him forgiveness for causing Him the loss of the sweet enchantment of His love toward us.

Do we let ourselves be worked by the divine hands, as the Humanity of Jesus Christ let Itself be worked? We must take everything that happens within ourselves, which is not sin, as divine crafting. If we do not do so, we deny the glory to the Father, we make divine life escape, and we lose sanctity. Everything we feel within ourselves - inspirations, mortifications, graces - is nothing other than a crafting of love. Do we take those things as God wants? Do we give Jesus the freedom to work, or by taking everything in a human manner and as meaningless, do we rather reject the divine crafting, forcing Him to bend His arms? Do we abandon ourselves in His arms as though we were dead in order to receive all the blows which the Lord will dispose for our sanctification?

My Love and my All, may your love inundate me everywhere, and burn all that is not yours. Let my love run always toward You, to burn away all that may sadden your Heart.

## Sixth Hour

From 10 to 11 PM

## Second Hour of Agony in the Garden of Gethsemani

O my sweet Jesus, one hour has already passed since You came to this Garden. Love took primacy over everything, making You suffer, all at once, everything which the executioners will make You suffer through the whole course of your most bitter Passion. Even more, Love compensates for it, and reaches the point of making You suffer what they cannot do to You, in the most interior parts of your Divine Person.

O my Jesus, I see You now staggering in your steps; yet, You want to walk. Tell me, O my Good, where do You want to go? Ah, I understand – to see your beloved disciples. I too want to accompany You, so that if You stagger, I may sustain You.

But, O my Jesus, another bitterness for your Heart: they are already sleeping. And You, always compassionate, call them, wake them up, and with love all paternal, admonish them and recommend to them vigil and prayer. Then You return to the Garden, but You carry another wound in your Heart. In that wound I see, Oh my Love, all the piercings of the consecrated souls who, because of temptation, mood, or lack of mortification, instead of clinging to You, keeping vigil and praying, abandon themselves to themselves and, sleepy, instead of making progress in love and in the union with You, draw back.

50

How much compassion I feel for You, oh passionate Lover; and I repair You for all the ingratitudes of your most faithful ones. These are the offenses which most sadden your adorable Heart, and their bitterness is such that they make You become delirious.

But, Oh Love without boundaries, your love which is already boiling in your veins, conquers everything and forgets everything. I see You prostrate to the ground as You pray, offer Yourself, repair and, in everything, try to glorify the Father for the offenses given to Him by creatures. I too, O my Jesus, prostrate myself with You, and with You I intend to do what You do.

But, O Jesus, delight of my heart, I see that crowds upon crowds, all sins, our miseries, our weaknesses, the most enormous crimes, the gravest ingratitudes, advance toward You, assail You, crush You, wound You, bite You. And You – what do You do? The Blood which boils in your veins comes to face all these offenses, bursts the veins open and pours out in large torrents; it makes You all wet, It flows to the ground, and You give Blood for offenses - life for death. Ah Love, to what a state I see You reduced! You are about to breathe your last. Oh, my Good, my sweet Life, O please, do not die! Raise your face from this ground, which You wet with your Most Holy Blood! Come into my arms! Let me die in your place!

But I hear the trembling and dying voice of my sweet Jesus, which says: "Father, if it be possible, let this chalice pass from Me; yet, not my will, but Yours be done."

It is now the second time I hear this from my sweet Jesus. But what do You make me understand from this "Father, if it be possible, let this chalice pass from Me"? O Jesus, all the rebellions of creatures advance toward You; You see that "Fiat Voluntas Tua", that "Your Will be done", which was to be the life of each creature, being rejected by almost all of them, and instead of finding life, they find death. And wanting to give life to all, and make a solemn reparation to the Father for the rebellions of creatures, as many as three times, You repeat: "Father, if it be possible, let this chalice pass from Me: that souls, withdrawing from Our Will, become lost. This chalice is very bitter for Me; however, not my will, but Yours be done."

But while You say this, your bitterness is so intense and so great, that You reach the extreme - You agonize, and are about to breathe your last.

O my Jesus, my Good, since You are in my arms, I too want to unite myself to You; I want to repair and compassionate You for all the faults and the sins committed against your Most Holy Will, and also pray to You that I may always do your Most Holy Will. May your Will be my breath, my air; may your Will be my heartbeat, my heart, my thought, my life and my death.

But, please, do not die! Where shall I go without You? To whom shall I turn? Who will give me help? Everything will end for me! O please, do not leave me, keep me as You want, as You best please, but keep me with You – always with You! May it never happen that I be separated from You, even for one instant! Rather, let me soothe You, repair You and compassionate You for all, as I see that all sins, of every kind, weigh upon You.

Therefore, my Love, I kiss your most holy head. But, what do I see? All the evil thoughts; and You feel disgust for them. For your most sacred head, each evil thought is a thorn which pricks You bitterly. Ah, the crown of thorns which the Jews will place upon You cannot be compared with these! How many crowns of thorns the evil thoughts of creatures place upon your adorable head, to the point that your Blood drips everywhere, from your forehead and from your hair! Jesus, I compassionate You, and would like to place upon You as many crowns of glory; and in order to soothe You, I offer You all the angelic intelligences and your own intelligence, to give You an act of compassion and of reparation for all.

O Jesus, I kiss your pitying eyes, and in them I see all the evil gazes of creatures, which make tears and blood flow over your face. I compassionate You, and I would like to soothe your sight by placing before You all the pleasures that can be found in Heaven and on earth through union of love with You.

Jesus, my Good, I kiss your most holy ears. But, what do I hear? I hear in them the echo of horrendous blasphemies, of shouts of revenge, and of malicious gossip. There is not one voice which does not resound in your most chaste hearing. Oh insatiable Love, I compassionate You, and I want to console You by making resound in it all the harmonies of Heaven, the most sweet voice of dear Mama, the ardent accents of Magdalene, and of all the loving souls.

Jesus, my Life, I want to impress a more fervent kiss on your face, whose beauty has no equal. Ah, this is the face on which the Angels, like cupids, desire to fix, for the great beauty that enraptures them. Yet, the creatures dirty it with spit, beat it with slaps, and trample it under foot. My Love, what daring! I would like to shout so loudly as to put them to flight! I compassionate You, and in order to repair for these insults, I go to the Most Holy Trinity, to ask for the kiss of the Father and of the Holy Spirit, and the divine caresses of Their creative hands. I also go to the Celestial Mama, that She may give me Her kisses, the caresses of Her maternal hands, and Her profound adorations; and I offer You everything, to repair for the offenses given to your most holy Face.

My sweet Good, I kiss your most holy mouth, embittered by horrible blasphemies, by the nausea of drunkenness and gluttony, by obscene discourses, by prayers done badly, by evil teachings, and by all the evil that man does with his tongue. Jesus, I compassionate You, and I want to sweeten your mouth by offering You all the angelic praises and the good use of the tongue made by many holy Christians.

My oppressed Love, I kiss your neck, and I see it loaded down with ropes and chains, because of the attachments and the sins of creatures. I compassionate You, and in order to relieve You, I offer You the indissoluble union of the Divine Persons; and fusing myself in this union, I extend my arms toward You, and forming a sweet chain of love around your neck, I want to remove the ropes of the attachments, which almost suffocate You; and to console You, I press You tightly to my heart.

Divine Fortress, I kiss your most holy shoulders. I see them lacerated, and your flesh almost torn to pieces by the scandals and the evil examples of creatures. I compassionate You, and in order to relieve You, I offer You your most holy examples, the examples of the Queen Mama, and those of all the saints. And I, O my Jesus, letting my kisses flow over each one of these wounds, want to enclose in them the souls who, by force of scandals, have been snatched from your Heart, and so re-join the flesh of your Most Holy Humanity.

My labored Jesus, I kiss your breast, which I see wounded by coldness, lukewarmness, lack of correspondence and ingratitudes of creatures. I compassionate You, and in order to relieve You, I offer You the reciprocal love of the Father and the Holy Spirit - the perfect correspondence of the Three Divine Persons. And plunging into your love, O my Jesus, I want to shelter You in order to reject the new blows that creatures throw at You with their sins; and taking your love, I want to wound them with it, that they may never again dare to offend You; and I want to pour it upon your breast, to soothe You and to heal You.

My Jesus, I kiss your creative hands. I see all the evil actions of creatures which, like as many nails, pierce your most holy hands. Therefore, You remain pierced, not with three nails, as on the Cross, but with as many nails for as many evil works as the creatures commit. I compassionate You, and to give You relief, I offer You all the holy works, and the courage of the martyrs in giving their blood and life for love of You. In sum, O my Jesus, I would like to offer You all the good works, in order to remove from You the many nails of the evil works.

O Jesus, I kiss your most holy feet, always untiring in searching for souls. In them You enclose all the steps of creatures; but You feel many of them run away, and You would want to stop them. At each of their evil steps, You feel a nail being driven into You, and You want to use their very nails in order to nail them to your love; and the pain You feel, and the effort You make in order to nail them to your love is so intense and so great, that You tremble all over. My God and my Good, I compassionate You, and in order to console You, I offer You the steps of the good religious and of all the faithful souls, who expose their lives in order to save souls.

O Jesus, I kiss your Heart. You continue to agonize, not for what the Jews will make You suffer, but for the pain which all the offenses of creatures cause You.

In these hours You want to give primacy to love, the second place to all sins, for which You expiate, repair, glorify the Father, and placate the Divine Justice; and the third to the Jews. In this way You show that the passion which the Jews will make You suffer will be nothing but the representation of the double, most bitter passion which love and sin make You suffer. And this is why I see, all concentrated in your Heart: the lance of love, the lance of sin; and you wait for the third one, the lance of the Jews. Your Heart, suffocated by love, suffers violent movements, impatient rushes of love, desires which consume You, and burning heartbeats, which would want to give life to every heart.

And it is exactly here, in your Heart, that You feel all the pain that creatures cause You, who, with their evil desires, disordered affections, profaned heartbeats, instead of wanting your love, look for other loves. Jesus, how much You suffer! I see You faint, submerged by the waves of our iniquities. I compassionate You, and I want to soothe the bitterness of your Heart, pierced three times, by offering You the eternal sweetnesses and the most sweet love of dear Mama Mary, as well as those of all your true lovers.

And now, O my Jesus, let my poor heart draw life from your Heart, that I may live only with your Heart; and in each offense You will receive, let me be ever ready to offer You a relief, a comfort, a reparation, an act of love, never interrupted.

## REFLECTIONS AND PRACTICES
## by St. Hannibal di Francia

In the second hour in Gethsemani, all sins from all times, past, present and future, present themselves before Jesus, and He loads upon Himself all these sins to give complete Glory to the Father. So, Jesus Christ expiated, prayed, and felt all our moods in His Heart without ever ceasing to pray. Do we always pray, in whatever mood we may be - cold, hard, tempted? Do we give Jesus the pains of our souls as reparation and relief in order to copy Him completely, thinking that each mood of ours is a pain of

Jesus? We must place it around Him as a pain of Jesus, to compassionate Him and relieve Him. And if possible we must say to Him: 'You have suffered too much. Take rest, and we will suffer in your place.'

Do we lose heart, or do we remain at the feet of Jesus with courage, giving Him all that we suffer, so that Jesus may find His own Humanity in us? That is, are we His Humanity for Jesus? What did the Humanity of Jesus do? It glorified Its Father, expiated, and pleaded the salvation of souls. And we - do we enclose within ourselves these three intentions of Jesus in everything we do, so as to be able to say, 'We enclose within ourselves all the Humanity of Jesus Christ'?

In our moments of darkness, do we place the intention of making the light of truth shine in others? And when we pray with fervor, do we place the intention of melting the ice of many hearts hardened in sin?

My Jesus, in order to compassionate You and relieve You from the total exhaustion in which You find Yourself, I rise up to Heaven and make your own Divinity my own; and placing It around You, I want to move all the offenses of creatures away from You. I want to offer You your Beauty to move the ugliness of sin away from You; your Sanctity to move away the horror of all those souls who make You feel repugnance, because they are dead to grace; your Peace to move the discords, the rebellions and the disturbances of all creatures away from You; your harmonies to relieve your hearing from the waves of many evil voices. My Jesus, I intend to offer You as many divine acts of reparation for as many offenses as assault You, almost wanting to give You death. I intend to give You life with your own acts. Then, O Jesus, I want to throw a wave of your Divinity upon all creatures, so that, at your divine contact, they may no longer dare to offend You.

Only in this way, O Jesus, will I be able to offer You compassion for all the offenses which You receive from creatures.

O Jesus, sweet Life of mine, may my prayers and my pains rise always toward Heaven, so as to let the light of grace rain upon all, and absorb your own Life in me.

# Seventh Hour

From 11 PM to Midnight

## Third Hour of Agony in the Garden of Gethsemani

My sweet Good, my heart can no longer bear it; I look at You and I see that You continue to agonize. Blood flows, in torrents, from all your body, and with such abundance, that unable to keep standing, You have fallen into a pool of it. O my Love, my heart breaks in seeing You so weak and exhausted! Your adorable Face and your creative hands lean into the ground and are smeared with blood. It seems to me that to the rivers of iniquities that creatures send You, You want to answer with rivers of blood, so that these sins may be drowned in it, and with it You may give to each one the deed of your forgiveness. But, please, O my Jesus, rise; what You suffer is too much. Let it be enough for your Love!

And while my lovable Jesus seems to be dying in His own Blood, Love gives Him new life. I see Him move with difficulty. He stands up, and soaked as He is with blood and mud, He seems to want to walk, but not having strength, He can barely drag Himself. Sweet Life of mine, let me carry You in my arms. Are You perhaps going to your dear disciples? But what is not the sorrow of your adorable Heart in finding them asleep again!

And You, with trembling and feeble voice, call them: "My sons, do not sleep! The hour is near. Do you not see how I have reduced Myself? Oh please, help Me, do not abandon Me in these extreme hours!"

And almost staggering, You are about to fall near them, while John extends his arms to sustain You. You are so unrecognizable that, if it wasn't for the tenderness and sweetness of your voice, they would not have recognized You. Then, recommending vigil and prayer to them, You return to the Garden, but with a second piercing to your Heart. In this piercing, my Good, I see all the sins of those souls who, in spite of the manifestations of your favors, in gifts, kisses and caresses, in the nights of trial, forgetting about your love and your gifts, have remained as though drowsy and sleepy, therefore losing the spirit of continuous prayer and of vigil.

My Jesus, it is yet true that after having seen You, after having enjoyed your gifts, when one is deprived of them, it takes great strength in order to persist. Only a miracle can allow these souls to endure the trial.

Therefore, as I compassionate You for these souls, whose negligences, fickleness and offenses are the most bitter for your Heart, I pray that, if they came to taking one single step which might slightly displease You, You will surround them with so much Grace as to stop them, so as not to lose the spirit of continuous prayer!

My sweet Jesus, as You return to the Garden, it seems You cannot take any more. You raise your face, soaked with Blood and earth, to Heaven, and You repeat for the third time: "Father, if it be possible, let this chalice pass from Me. Holy Father, help Me! I need comfort! It is true that because of the sins which weigh upon Me, I am nauseating, repugnant, the least among men, before your infinite Majesty; your Justice is angry with Me – but look at Me, O Father, I am always your Son, who forms one single thing with You. Oh please, help - pity, O Father! Do not leave Me without comfort!"

Then, O my sweet Good, I seem to hear You call your dear Mama to your help: "Sweet Mama, hold Me in your arms, as You did when I was a Child! Give Me that milk which I suckled from You, to refresh Me and to sweeten the bitternesses of my agony. Give Me your Heart, which formed all my contentment. My Mama, Magdalene, dear Apostles, all of you who love Me – help Me, comfort Me! Do not leave Me alone in these extreme moments; gather all around Me like a crown; give Me the comfort of your company, of your love!"

Jesus, my Love, who can resist in seeing You in these extreme conditions? What heart would ever be so hard as not to break in seeing You so drowned in Blood? Who would not pour bitter tears in torrents, upon hearing your sorrowful accents, looking for help and comfort?

My Jesus, be consoled, I now see that the Father sends You an Angel as comfort and help, that You may leave this state of agony and give Yourself into the hands of the Jews. And while You are with the Angel, I will go around Heaven and earth. You will allow me to take this Blood that You have shed, that I may give It to all men, as pledge of salvation for each one, and bring You as comfort and in exchange, their affections, heartbeats, thoughts, steps and works.

My Celestial Mama, I come to You in order to go to all souls, to give to them the Blood of Jesus. Sweet Mama, Jesus wants comfort, and the greatest comfort we can give Him is to bring Him souls.

Magdalene, accompany us! All of you, Angels, come and see how Jesus is reduced! He wants comfort from all, and His state of exhaustion is such that He refuses no one.

My Jesus, while You drink the chalice full of intense bitternesses, which the Celestial Father has sent You, I hear You sigh, moan, rave more, and with suffocated voice, You say: "Souls, souls, come, relieve Me! Take a place in my Humanity; I want you, I long for you! O please, do not be deaf to my voices; do not render vain my ardent desires, my Blood, my Love, my pains! Come, souls, come!"

Delirious Jesus, each one of your moans and sighs is a wound to my heart, which gives me no peace. So I make your Blood, your Will, your ardent zeal, your Love, my own, and wandering around Heaven and earth, I want to go through all souls, to give them your Blood as a pledge for their salvation, and bring them to You, to calm your restlessness, your delirium, and to sweeten the bitternesses of your agony. And while I do this, You, accompany me with your gaze.

My Mama, I come to You, because Jesus wants souls – He wants comfort. Therefore, give me your maternal hand, and let us go around together, throughout the whole world, searching for souls. Let us enclose in His Blood the affections, the desires, the thoughts, the works, the steps of all creatures, and let us throw the flames of His Heart into their souls, that they may surrender, and so, enclosed in His Blood and transformed within His flames, we will bring them around Jesus, to soothe the pains of His most bitter agony.

My guardian Angel, precede us; go and dispose the souls who must receive this Blood, so that not one drop may remain without its abundant effect. My Mama, hurry, let us go around! I see the gaze of Jesus that follows us; I hear His repeated sobs, pushing us to hasten our task.

And here we are, Mama, at the first steps, already at the door of the houses where the sick are lying. How many tormented limbs; how many, in the atrocity of the spasms, burst into blasphemies and try to take their own lives away. Others are abandoned by all, and have no one who would offer them a word of comfort, the most necessary aids, and so they swear and despair even more. Ah, Mama, I hear the sobs of Jesus, who sees, repaid with offenses, the dearest predilections of love, which make the souls suffer in order to render them similar to Him. O please, let us give them His Blood, that It may administer to them the necessary aids, and with Its light, It may make them understand the good which is in suffering and the likeness to Jesus they acquire. And You, my Mama, place Yourself near them, and as affectionate mother, touch their suffering limbs with your maternal hands; soothe their pains; take them in your arms, and pour from your Heart torrents of graces over all of their pains. Keep company with the abandoned; console the afflicted. For those who lack the necessary means, dispose generous souls to help them; for those who find themselves under the atrocity of the spasms, impetrate respite and rest, so that, relieved, they may bear with more patience whatever Jesus disposes for them.

Let us continue to go around, and let us enter into the rooms of the dying. My Mama what terror! How many souls are about to fall into hell! How many, after a life of sin, want to give the last sorrow to that Heart, repeatedly pierced, by crowning their last breath with an act of desperation. Many demons are around them, striking into their hearts terror and fright of the divine judgments, and therefore wage against them the final assault, to lead them to hell. They would want to unleash the infernal flames in order to enwrap them, and therefore prevent the rising of hope. Others, entangled by the bonds of the earth, are unable to resign themselves to take the last step. Please, O Mama, these moments are extreme, they need much help. Don't You see how they tremble, how they wriggle about in the midst of the spasms of agony, how they ask for help and for pity? The earth has already disappeared for them! Holy Mama, place your maternal hand upon their ice-cold forehead; receive their last breaths. Let us give the Blood of Jesus to each of the dying, so that, putting the demons to flight, It may dispose them all to receive the last Sacraments, and to a good and holy death. For comfort, let us give them the agonies of Jesus, His kisses, His tears, His wounds. Let us tear the laces which keep them entangled; let us make everyone hear the word of forgiveness, and let us place such confidence in their hearts, as to make them fling themselves into the arms of Jesus. When Jesus judges them, He will find them covered with His own Blood, abandoned in His arms, and so He will give His forgiveness to all.

Let us continue to go around, O Mama. Let your maternal gaze look with love upon the earth, and be moved to compassion for many poor creatures who need this Blood. My Mama, I feel pushed to run by the searching gaze of Jesus, because He wants souls. I hear His moans in the depth of my heart, repeating to me: "My child, help Me, give Me souls!"

But see, O Mama, how the earth is filled with souls who are about to fall into sin, and Jesus bursts into crying in seeing His Blood suffer new profanations. It would take a miracle to prevent their fall; therefore, let us give them the Blood of Jesus, that they may find in It the strength and the grace not to fall into sin.

One more step, O Mama, and here are the souls already fallen into guilt, who would like a hand in order to stand up again. Jesus loves them, but He looks at them with horror, because they are covered with mud, and His agony becomes more intense. Let us give them the Blood of Jesus, that they may find the hand which raises them up again. See O Mama, these are souls who need this Blood – souls who are dead to grace. Oh, how deplorable is their state! Heaven looks at them and cries with sorrow; the earth fixes on them with disgust; all the elements are against them and would want to destroy them, because they are enemies of the Creator. Please, O Mama, the Blood of Jesus contains life, so let us give It to them, so that, at Its touch, these souls may rise again - and may rise again more beautiful, so as to make all Heaven and all earth smile.

Let us continue to wander, O Mama. See, there are souls who carry the mark of perdition; souls who sin and run away from Jesus; who offend Him and despair of His forgiveness. These are the new Judases, spread throughout the earth, who pierce that Heart, so embittered. Let us give them the Blood of Jesus, that It may erase from them the mark of perdition, and impress that of salvation. May It place in their hearts such confidence and love after sin, as to make them run to the feet of Jesus, and cling to those divine feet, never to detach from them again.

See, O Mama, there are souls who are hurling themselves toward perdition, and there is no one to arrest their race. O please, let us place this Blood before their feet, so that, at Its touch, at Its light, and at Its supplicating voices which want to save them, they may draw back and place themselves on the path of salvation!

Let us continue to go around, O Mama. See, there are good souls, innocent souls, in whom Jesus finds His delights and His rest in creation. But creatures are around them with many snares and scandals, to snatch this innocence away, and to turn the delights and rest of Jesus into crying and bitternesses, as if they had no other aim than to cause continuous sorrows to that Divine Heart. So, let us seal and surround their innocence with the Blood of Jesus, like a wall of defense, so that sin may not enter into them. With It, put to flight whomever wanted to contaminate them, and preserve them spotless and pure, so that Jesus may find, through them, His rest in creation and all His delights; and for love of them, He may be moved to pity for many other poor creatures. My Mama, let us place these souls in the Blood of Jesus; let us bind them, and bind them all over, with the Holy Will of God; let us place them in His arms, and let us bind them to His Heart with the sweet chains of His love, in order to soothe the bitternesses of His mortal agony.

But listen, O Mama, this Blood cries out and wants yet more souls. Let us run together, and let us go to the regions of the heretics and of the unbelievers. How much sorrow does Jesus not feel in these regions. He, who is the life of all, receives not even a tiny act of love in return; He is not known by His very creatures. Please, O Mama, let us give them this Blood, that It may cast away the darkness of ignorance and of heresy. Let them comprehend that they have a soul, and open the Heavens for them. Then, let us place them all in the Blood of Jesus; let us lead them around Him, like many orphaned and exiled children, who find their Father; and so Jesus will feel comforted in His most bitter agony.

But Jesus seems to be not yet satisfied, because He wants yet more souls. He feels the dying souls of these regions being snatched from His arms, to fall into hell. These souls are now about to breathe their last and fall into the abyss. No one is near them to save them. Time is short, the moments are extreme – they will certainly be lost! No, Mama, this Blood will not be shed uselessly for them; therefore, let us quickly fly to them; let us pour the Blood of Jesus over their heads, that It may serve them as baptism and infuse in them faith, hope and love. Place Yourself near them, O Mama; make up for all that they lack. Even more, make Yourself seen. On your face shines the beauty of Jesus; your manners are all similar to His; and so, in seeing You, they will certainly be able to know Jesus. Then, press them to your maternal Heart; infuse in them the life of Jesus, which You possess; tell them that, as their Mother, You want them to be happy forever, with You in Heaven; and as they breathe their last, receive them into your arms, and let them pass from yours into those of Jesus. And if Jesus, according to the rights of Justice, will show He does not want to receive them, remind Him of the love with which He entrusted them to You at the foot of the Cross. Claim your rights as mother, so that He will not be able to resist your love and prayers, and while making your Heart content, He will also content His ardent desires.

And now, O Mama, let us take this Blood and let us give It to all: to the afflicted, that they may receive comfort; to the poor, that they may suffer resigned to their poverty; to those who are tempted, that they may obtain victory; to the disbelieving, that the virtue of Faith may triumph in them; to the blasphemers, that they may turn the blasphemies into benedictions; to the priests, that they may understand their mission and be worthy ministers of Jesus. With this Blood, touch their lips, that they may say no words which are not of glory to God; touch their feet, that they may let them fly to go in search for souls to lead to Jesus.

Let us give this Blood to the leaders of the peoples, that they may be united among them, and feel meekness and love for their subjects.

Let us fly now into Purgatory, and let us give It also to the purging souls, because they so much cry for and claim this Blood for their liberation. Don't You hear, O Mama, their moans, the fidgets of love, the tortures, and how they feel continuously drawn to the Highest Good? See how Jesus Himself wants to purge them more quickly in order to have them with Himself. He attracts them with His love, and they requite Him with continuous surges toward Him. But as they find themselves in His presence, unable to yet sustain the purity of His divine gaze, they are forced to draw back and to plunge again into the flames!

My Mama, let us descend into this profound prison, and pouring this Blood over them, let us bring them light; let us calm their fidgets of love; let us dampen the fire that burns them; let us purify their stains; and so, free of every pain, they will fly into the arms of the Highest Good. Let us give this Blood to the most abandoned souls, that they may find in It all the suffrages that creatures deny to them. To all, O Mama, let us give this Blood; let us not deprive any of them, so that, by virtue of It, all may find relief and liberation. Be Queen in these regions of crying and of lamentations; extend your maternal hands and, one by one, take them out of these ardent flames, and allow them all to take flight toward Heaven. And now, we too, let us fly toward Heaven; let us place ourselves at the gates of eternity and allow me, O Mama, to give this Blood also to You, for your greater glory. May this Blood inundate You with new light and with new contentments. And let this light descend for the good of all creatures, to give graces and salvation to all.

My Mama, give this Blood also to me; You know how much I need It. With your own maternal hands, retouch me completely with this Blood; and while retouching me, purify my stains, heal my wounds, enrich my poverty; let this Blood circulate in my veins and give me again all the life of Jesus. May It descend into my heart, and transform it into His very Heart; may It embellish me so much that Jesus may find all His contentments in me. Finally, O Mama, let us enter the celestial regions, and let us give this Blood to all the Saints, to all the Angels, that they may receive greater glory, burst into thanksgivings to Jesus, and pray for us, that we may reach them, by virtue of this Blood. And after having given this Blood to all, let us go to Jesus again. Angels, Saints, come with us. Ah, He sighs for souls; He wants to let them all enter His Humanity, to give to all the fruits of His Blood. Let us place them around Him, and He will feel restored to life, and repaid for the most bitter agony He has suffered. And now, Holy Mama, let us call all the elements to keep Him company, that they too may give honor to Jesus.

O light of the sun, come to dispel the darkness of this night, to give comfort to Jesus. O stars, with your flickering rays, descend from heaven; come and give comfort to Jesus. Flowers of the earth, come with your fragrances; birds, come with your warblings; all elements of the earth, come to comfort Jesus. Come, O sea, to refresh and wash Jesus. He is our Creator, our life, our All; come all of you to comfort Him, to pay Him homage as our Sovereign Lord. But – ah, Jesus does not look for light, stars, flowers, birds...He wants souls – souls! Here they are, O my sweet Good, all together with me. Your dear Mama is close to You - please rest in Her arms; She too will receive comfort by pressing You to Her womb, because She greatly shared in your sorrowful agony.

Magdalene also is here; Mary is here, and all the loving souls of all centuries. Please, O Jesus, accept them, and say a word of forgiveness and of love to all. Bind them all to your love, so that not one more soul may escape You!

But – ah, it seems to me that You say: "O child, how many souls escape Me by force, and fall into eternal ruin! So, how can my sorrow ever be soothed, if I love one single soul so much - as much as I love all souls together?"

Agonizing Jesus, it seems that your life is extinguishing. I already hear the rattle of agony, your beautiful eyes eclipsed by the nearness of death, all of your limbs abandoned; and often it seems that You no longer breathe. I feel my heart burst with pain. I hug You and I feel You ice-cold. I shake You and You give no sign of life! Jesus, are You dead? Afflicted Mama, Angels of Heaven, come to cry over Jesus, and do not permit that I continue to live without Him. Ah, I cannot! I press Him more tightly to myself, and I hear Him taking another breath - and then, again, He gives no sign of life! I call Him: "Jesus, Jesus, my Life, do not die!"

But I already hear the clamor of your enemies, who are coming to take You. Who will defend You in your state? But here You are, stirring Yourself as though rising again from death to life, looking at me, saying: "O soul, are you here? Have you then been spectator of my pains and of the so many deaths I suffered? Know that in these three hours of most bitter agony in the Garden, I enclosed in Myself all the lives of creatures, and I suffered all of their pains, and their very death, giving my own life to each one of them. My agonies will sustain theirs; my bitternesses

72

and my death will turn into a fount of sweetness and life for them. How much souls cost Me! Were I at least requited! You have seen that while I was dying, I would return to breathe again: those were the deaths of the creatures that I felt within Me!"

My panting Jesus, since You also wanted to enclose my life in You, and therefore also my death, I pray You, for this most bitter agony of yours, to come to my assistance at the moment of my death. I have given You my heart as refuge and rest, my arms to sustain You, and all of my being at your disposal; and – oh, how gladly I would give myself into the hands of your enemies, to die in your place! Come, O life of my heart, at that moment, to return to me all I have given You: your company, your Heart as bed and rest, your arms as support, your labored breath to alleviate my labors; in such a way that, in breathing, I will breathe through your breath which, like purifying air, will purify me of any stain, and will dispose me to enter the eternal beatitude.

Even more, my sweet Jesus, then You will give your very Most Holy Humanity to my soul, so that, in looking at me, You may see me through Yourself; and in looking at Yourself, You may find nothing for which to judge me. Then You will bathe me in your Blood; You will clothe me with the candid garment of your Most Holy Will; You will adorn me with your Love, and giving me the last kiss, You will let me take flight from earth unto Heaven. And what I want for myself, do it for all the agonizing; clasp them all in your embrace of love, and giving them the kiss of their union with You, save them all and allow no one to be lost!

My afflicted Good, I offer You this holy Hour in memory of your Passion and Death, to disarm the just wrath of God for the so many sins, for the triumph of the Holy Church, for the conversion of all sinners, for peace among peoples, especially our country, for our sanctification, and in suffrage for the purging souls.

But I see that your enemies are near, and You want to leave me in order to go toward them. Jesus, allow me to offer You all the holy kisses of your Most Holy Mother; let me kiss those lips, which Judas is about to dare to kiss with his infernal kiss. Let me dry your Face, wet with Blood, and upon which slaps and spit are about to pour. I cling tightly to your Heart, I do not leave You – I will follow You. And You, bless me and assist me. Amen

## REFLECTIONS AND PRACTICES
## by St. Hannibal di Francia

In this third hour of Gethsemani, Jesus asked for help from Heaven. His pains were so many that He also asked for the comfort of His disciples. And we - do we always ask for help from Heaven in any painful circumstance? And if we turn also to creatures, do we do this with order, and with those who can comfort us in a saintly way? Are we at least resigned, if we do not receive those comforts which we were hoping for, using the indifference of creatures to abandon ourselves more in the arms of Jesus? Jesus was comforted by an Angel. And we - can we say that we are the angels of Jesus by remaining around Him to comfort Him and share in His bitterness? However, in order to be as a true angel for Jesus, it is necessary to take sufferings as sent by Him, and therefore as divine sufferings. Only then can we dare to console a God so embittered. Otherwise, if we take pains in a human

74

way, we cannot use them to comfort this Man-God, and therefore we cannot be His angels.

In the pains which Jesus sends to us, it seems that He sends us the chalice in which we must place the fruit of those pains. These pains, suffered with love and resignation, will turn into a most sweet nectar for Jesus. In every pain we will say: 'Jesus is calling us around Him to be His angel. He wants our comforts, so He makes us share in His pains.'

My love, Jesus, in my pains I look for your Heart to rest, and in your pains I intend to give You shelter with my pains, so that we may exchange them, and I may be your consoling angel.

# Eighth Hour

From Midnight to 1 AM

## Jesus is arrested

O my Jesus, it is already midnight. You feel that your enemies are drawing near; tidying Yourself up and drying up your Blood, strengthened by the comforts received, You go to your disciples again. You call them, You admonish them, and You take them with You, as You go to meet your enemies, wanting to repair, with your promptness, my slowness, indolence and laziness in working and suffering for love of You.

But, O sweet Jesus, my Good, what a touching scene I see! You first meet the perfidious Judas, who, drawing near You and throwing his arms around your neck, greets You and kisses You. And You, most passionate Love, do not disdain to kiss those infernal lips; You embrace him and press him to your Heart, wanting to snatch him from hell, and giving him signs of new love. My Jesus, how is it possible not to love You? The tenderness of your love is such that it should snatch every heart to love You; yet, they do not love You! And You, O my Jesus, in bearing this kiss of Judas, repair for the betrayals, the pretenses, the deceptions under the aspect of friendship and sanctity, especially of priests. Your kiss, then, shows that, not to one sinner, provided that he comes humbled before You, would You refuse your forgiveness.

My most tender Jesus, You now give Yourself into the hands of the enemies, giving them the power to make You suffer whatever they want. I too, O my Jesus, give myself into your hands, that You may do with me, freely, whatever You best please; and together with You, I want to follow your Will, your reparations, and suffer your pains. I want to be always around You, that there may be no offense which I do not repair; no bitterness which I do not soothe; no spit or blows that You receive, which are not followed by one kiss and caress of mine. In the falls You will suffer, my hands will always be ready to help You in order to lift You. So, I want to be always with You, O my Jesus; I do not want to leave You alone even for one minute. And to be more certain, place me inside of Yourself, and I will be in your mind, in your gazes, in your Heart, and in all of You, so that whatever You do, I may do as well. In this way, I will be able to keep You faithful company, and nothing of your pains will escape me, in order to give You my return of love for everything.

My sweet Good, I will be at your side to defend You, to learn your teachings, to count, one by one, all of your words. Ah, how sweetly does the word with which You addressed Judas, descend into my heart: "Friend, why have you come?" And I feel that You address me too with the same word - not calling me friend, but by the sweet name of child: "Child, why have you come?"; to hear me answer: "Jesus – to love You". "Why have you come?", You repeat to me when I wake up in the morning; "Why have you come?", if I pray; "Why have you come?", You repeat to me in the Holy Host, if I come to receive You into my heart.

What a beautiful call for me and for all! But how many, to your "Why have you come?", answer: "I come to offend You!" Others, pretending not to hear You, give themselves to all kinds of sins, and answer your "Why have you come?", by going to hell! How much compassion I feel for You, O my Jesus! I would like to take the very ropes with which your enemies are about to bind You, in order to bind these souls and spare You this sorrow.

But, again, I hear your most tender voice which says, as You go to meet your enemies: "Who are you looking for?" And they answer: "Jesus the Nazarene". And You, to them: "It is I". With only this word You say everything, and You let Yourself be known for who You are; so much so, that the enemies tremble and fall to the ground, as though dead. And You, Love which has no equal, repeating again, "It is I", call them back to life and You give Yourself, on your own, into the power of the enemies. Perfidious and ungrateful, instead of falling to your feet, humbled and palpitating,

to ask for your forgiveness, taking advantage of your goodness and despising your graces and prodigies, they lay hands on You, they bind You with ropes and chains, they grip You, they cast You to the ground, they trample upon You, they tear your hair. And You, with unheard-of patience, remain silent, suffering and repairing for the offenses of those who, in spite of miracles, do not surrender to your Grace, and become more obstinate.

With those ropes and chains, You impetrate from the Father the grace to snap the chains of our sins, and You bind us with the sweet chain of love. And, lovingly, You correct Peter, who wants to defend You to the point of cutting off the ear of Malchus. With this, You intend to repair for the good works, which are not done with holy prudence, or which fall into sin because of excessive zeal.

My most patient Jesus, it seems that these ropes and chains give something more beautiful to your Divine Person: your forehead becomes more majestic, so much so, as to draw the attention of your enemies themselves; your eyes blaze with more light; your Divine Face assumes a supreme peace and sweetness, such as to enamor your very executioners. With your sweet and penetrating accents, though few, You make them tremble; so much so, that if they dare to offend You, it is because You Yourself allow them to do so.

Oh chained and bound Love, can You ever allow Yourself to be bound for me, making a greater display of your love toward me, while I, your little child, remain without chains? No, no; rather, with your most holy hands, bind me with your own ropes and chains.

Therefore I pray You, as I kiss your divine forehead, to bind all of my thoughts, my eyes, my ears, my tongue, my heart, my affections, and all of me; and together with me, bind all creatures, so that, in feeling the sweetnesses of your loving chains, they may never again dare to offend You.

My sweet Good, it is now one o'clock. My mind begins to doze off. I will do the best I can in order to stay awake; but if sleep surprises me, I leave myself inside of You, in order to follow whatever You do; even more, You Yourself will do it for me. In You I leave my thoughts, to defend You from your enemies; my breathing, as cortege and company; my heartbeat, to tell You, constantly, that I love You and to make up for the love which others do not give You; the drops of my blood, to repair You and to render back to You the honor and the esteem which they will take away from You with insults, spit and slaps. My Jesus, bless me and let me sleep in your adorable Heart; and from your heartbeats, accelerated by love or by sorrow, I will be able to wake up often, so as not to interrupt our company. Let us make this agreement, O Jesus!

## REFLECTIONS AND PRACTICES
## by St. Hannibal di Francia

Jesus promptly gave Himself into the hands of the enemies, seeing the Will of the Father in His enemies.

In the deceptions, in the betrayals of creatures, are we ready to forgive as Jesus forgave? Do we take from the hands of God all the evil that we receive from creatures? Are we ready to do all that Jesus wants from us? In the crosses, in the strains, can we say that our patience imitates that of Jesus?

My chained Jesus, may your chains bind my heart and keep it still, to make it ready to suffer everything You want.

# Ninth Hour

From 1 to 2 AM

## Thrown from a ledge, Jesus falls
## into the Cedron stream

My beloved Good, my poor mind follows You between vigil and sleep. How can I leave myself prey to sleep, when I see that everyone leaves You and runs away from You? The Apostles themselves, the fervent Peter, who a little while ago said he wanted to give his life for You; the beloved disciple whom, with so much love, You allowed to rest upon your Heart – ah, they all abandon You, and leave You at the mercy of your cruel enemies!

My Jesus, You are alone! Your most pure eyes look around to see if at least one of those favored by You is following You to prove to You his love and to defend You. And as You see that no one

– no one has remained faithful to You, your Heart catches, and You burst into crying. You feel more pain for the abandonment of your most faithful ones, than for what the very enemies are doing to You. My Jesus, do not cry; or rather, let me cry together with You. And lovable Jesus seems to say: "Ah, child, let us cry together over the lot of so many souls consecrated to Me, who, over little trials, over incidents of life, no longer take care of Me and leave Me alone; for many others, timid and cowardly, who, for lack of courage and trust, abandon Me; for many upon many who, not finding their own advantage in holy things, do not care about Me; for many priests who

81

preach, who celebrate, who confess for love of interest and of self-glory. These show that they are around Me, but I remain always alone! Ah, child, how hard is this abandonment for Me! Not only do my eyes cry, but my Heart bleeds! O please, I beg you to repair my bitter pain by promising that you will not leave Me alone."

Yes, O my Jesus, I promise, helped by your grace, identifying myself with your Divine Will. But, O Jesus, while You cry over the abandonment of your dear ones, the enemies spare no outrage that they can do to You. Gripped and bound as You are, O my Good, to the point that You cannot even take a step by Yourself, they trample on You; they drag You along those ways full of rocks and thorns, such that there is no movement which does not make You knock against the rocks and be pricked by the thorns. Ah, my Jesus, I see that as they drag You, You leave behind Yourself your precious Blood, and your golden hair which they tear from your head! My Life and my All, allow me to gather it, that I may bind all the steps of creatures who do not spare You even at nighttime; rather, they use the night to offend You more – some for gatherings, some for pleasures, some for theatricals, some for committing sacrilegious thefts! My Jesus, I unite myself to You in order to repair for all these offenses.

But, O my Jesus, we are now at the Cedron stream, and the perfidious Jews prepare to throw You into it. They make You bump against a rock which is there, with such violence as to make You shed most precious Blood from your mouth, with which You mark that rock! Then, pulling You, they cast You down into those putrid waters, in such a way that these enter into your ears, into your mouth, into your nostrils. Oh, unreachable love, You remain inundated and as though wrapped by those putrid, nauseating and cold waters. In this way, You represent, vividly, the heart-rending state of creatures when they commit sin! Oh, how they remain covered, inside and out, by a mantle of filth, such as to be disgusting to Heaven and to whomever can see them, therefore attracting the lightnings of Divine Justice upon themselves! Oh, Life of my life, can there ever be greater love? In order to remove from us this mantle of filth, You allow your enemies to throw You into this stream, and You suffer everything to repair for the sacrileges and the coldness of the souls who receive You sacrilegiously, and who, more than the stream, force You to enter into their hearts, and to make You feel all of their nausea! You also permit that these waters penetrate deep into your bowels; so much so, that the enemies, fearing that You may be drowned, in order to spare You for greater torments, lift You up. But You are so disgusting that they themselves feel nauseated to touch You.

My tender Jesus, You are now out of the stream. My heart cannot bear seeing You so wettened by those nauseating waters. I see You shivering from head to foot because of the cold. You look around, searching with your eyes, what You cannot do with your voice, for one at least who would dry You, clean You and warm You. But, in vain – no one is moved to pity for You: the enemies mock You and deride You; your own have abandoned You; your sweet Mama is far away, because the Father so disposes!

Here I am, O Jesus - come into my arms. I want to cry so much as to form a bath for You in order to wash You, clean You, and with my hands, fix your hair, which is all disheveled. My Love, I want to enclose You in my heart to warm You with the warmth of my affections; I want to perfume You with my holy desires; I want to repair for all these offenses, and place my life together with Yours, in order to save all souls. I want to offer You my heart as a place of rest, to be able to somehow relieve You from the pains You have suffered up to now; and then, we will continue together the way of your Passion.

## REFLECTIONS AND PRACTICES
## by St. Hannibal di Francia

In this hour Jesus abandoned Himself at the mercy of His enemies, who reached the point of throwing Him into the Cedron stream. But the Humanity of Jesus looked at all of them with love, bearing everything for love of them.

And we - do we abandon ourselves at the mercy of the Will of God? In our weaknesses and falls, are we ready to stand up again to throw ourselves into the arms of Jesus? Tormented Jesus was thrown into the Cedron stream, feeling suffocation, nausea and repugnance. And we - do we abhor any stain and shadow of sin? Are we ready to give shelter to Jesus in our heart, so as not to make Him feel the nausea which other souls give Him with sin, and to compensate for the nausea that we ourselves have given Him many times?

My tormented Jesus, do not spare me in anything, and let me be the object of your divine and loving aims!

# Tenth Hour

From 2 to 3 AM

## Jesus is presented to Annas

Jesus, be always with me. Sweet Mama, let us follow Jesus together. My Jesus, Divine Sentry, watching over me in your Heart, and not wanting to remain alone without me, You wake me up and let me be present with You in the house of Annas.

You are now at the moment in which Annas questions You about your doctrine and your disciples. And You, O Jesus, in order to defend the glory of the Father, open your most sacred mouth, and with sonorous and dignified voice, answer: "I have spoken in public, and all those here present have heard Me."

At your dignified accents, all feel trembling, but their perfidy is such that a servant, wanting to honor Annas, comes close to You and with a fierce hand gives You a slap, but so violent as to make You stagger, and to bruise your most holy Face.

Now I understand, my sweet Life, why You woke me up. You were right; who would sustain You at this moment, as You are about to fall? Your enemies burst into satanic laughter, whistling and clapping, applauding an act so unjust. And You, staggering, have no one to lean on. My

Jesus, I hug You; even more, I want to form a wall with my being and I offer You my cheek with courage, ready to bear any suffering for love of You. I compassionate You for this outrage, and together with You I repair for the fearfulness of many souls, who get easily discouraged. I repair for all those who, out of fear, do not speak the truth; for the lack of respect due to priests, and for murmuring.

But, my afflicted Jesus, I see that Annas sends You to Caiphas. Your enemies hurl You down the stairs, and You, my Love, in this painful fall repair for those who at nighttime fall into sin under the favor of darkness, and You call the heretics and the unbelievers to the light of Faith.

I too want to follow You in these reparations, and on the way to Caiphas, I send You my sighs in order to defend You from your enemies. While I sleep, continue to be my sentry, and wake me up whenever You need to. Give me your kiss and your blessing, and I kiss your Heart, and in It I continue my sleep.

## REFLECTIONS AND PRACTICES
## by St. Hannibal di Francia

Jesus, brought before Annas, is questioned by him about His doctrine and about His disciples. He answers about His doctrine in order to glorify the Father, but He does not touch His disciples so as not to fail in Charity. And we - are we intrepid and courageous when it comes to glorifying the Lord, or do we let ourselves be won by human respect? We must always say the truth, even in front of distinguished people. In our speaking, do we always look for the glory of God? In order to exalt the glory of God, do we bear everything with patience like Jesus? Do we always avoid speaking ill of our neighbor, and do we excuse him if we hear that others run him down? Jesus watches over our hearts. Do we watch over the Heart of Jesus, so that He may not receive any offense which has not been repaired by us? Do we watch over ourselves in everything, so that each one of our thoughts, gazes, words, affections, heartbeats and desires may be as many sentries around Jesus, watching over His Heart, and repairing for all the offenses? And in order to do this, do we pray Jesus to watch over each one of our acts, and to help us to watch over our own hearts? Every act that we do in God is a divine life that we take within ourselves. And since we are very limited, while God is immense, we cannot enclose a God in our simple act. Therefore, let us multiply them as much as we can in order to at least enlarge our capacity of understanding and love. Are we ready to answer when our Jesus calls us? The call from God can make itself heard in many ways: with inspirations, with the reading of good books, by example. It can make itself heard tangibly with the attractions of grace, and even with the very intemperances of the air.

My sweet Jesus, may your voice resound always in my heart; may everything that surrounds me, inside and out, be the continuous voice which calls me to love You always; and may the harmony of your divine voice prevent me from hearing any other distractive human voice.

# Eleventh Hour

From 3 to 4 AM

## Jesus in the house of Caiphas

My afflicted and abandoned Good, while my weak nature sleeps in your sorrowful Heart, my sleep is often interrupted by the pangs of love and sorrow of your Divine Heart. Between vigil and sleep, I hear the blows that they give You, so I wake up and I say: My poor Jesus, abandoned by everyone! There is no one who takes your part. But from within your Heart I offer You my life as support for You, as they knock You about. And I fall asleep again; but another pang of love of your Divine Heart wakes me up, and I am deafened by the insults that they send You, by the whispering, the shouting and the running of people.

My Love, how is it that they are all against You? What have You done that they want to tear You to pieces like many rabid wolves? I feel my blood freeze in hearing the preparations of your enemies, and I tremble in anguish thinking of what to do in order to defend You.

But my afflicted Jesus, keeping me in His Heart, squeezes me more tightly, and says to me: "My child, I have done nothing wrong, and I have done everything: mine is the crime of love, which contains all sacrifices, and love of immeasurable cost. We are still at the beginning; remain in my Heart, observe everything, love Me, be silent, and learn. Let your ice-cold blood flow in my veins so as to

88

refresh my Blood which is all in flames. Let your trembling flow within my limbs, so that, being identified with Me, you may be strengthened and warmed in order to feel part of my pains, and you may also acquire strength in seeing Me suffer so much. This will be the most beautiful defense that you can make for Me. Be faithful to Me, and be attentive."


Sweet Love of mine, the clamor of your enemies is so intense and so great that I can no longer sleep. The shoves become more violent. I hear the noise of the chains with which they bound You, and so tightly as to make living blood ooze from your wrists, with which You mark those streets. Remember that my blood is in Yours, and as You shed It, mine kisses It, adores It and repairs It. May your Blood be light to all those who offend You at night, and a magnet to draw all hearts around You, my Love and my All.


While they drag You, the air seems to be deafened by shouts and whistles. And You arrive before Caiphas. You are all meek, modest, humble; your sweetness and patience is such as to terrorize even your enemies; and Caiphas, full of rage, would want to devour You. Ah, how well can Innocence and sin be distinguished!


My Love, You are before Caiphas as the most guilty, in the act of being condemned. Caiphas asks the witnesses what your crimes are. Ah, he should rather have asked what is your love! And some accuse You of one thing, some of another, speaking nonsense and contradicting themselves. As they accuse You, the soldiers who are near You tear your hair, and unload horrible slaps on your most holy Face, such as to resound through the whole room; they twist your lips, they hit You, while You remain silent and suffer. And if You look at them, the light of your eyes descends into their hearts, and unable to sustain it, they move away from You. But others take their place, to make of You a greater slaughter.

But in the midst of many accusations and offenses, I see You pricking up your ears. Your Heart beats strongly, and is about to burst with pain. Tell me, my afflicted Good, what is it? I see that your love is so great that You anxiously await that which your enemies are doing to You, and You offer it for our salvation. In total calm, your Heart repairs for slanders, hatred, false witnessings, and for the evil done to innocents with premeditation; and You repair for those who offend You upon the instigation of leaders, and for the offenses of the ecclesiastics. And while I am united with You, following your own reparations, I feel a change in You - from a new sorrow, never before felt. Tell me, tell me, what is it? Share everything with me, O Jesus.

"Child, do you want to know? I hear the voice of Peter who says he does not know Me. Then he swore, and then, again, he perjured and anathematized knowing Me. O Peter, what! You do not know Me? Don't you remember with how many gifts I filled you? Ah, if others make Me die of pains, you make Me die of sorrow! Ah, how wrong it was of you to follow Me from a distance, and so expose yourself to the occasions!"

My denied Good, how quickly the offenses of your dearest ones can be recognized! O Jesus, I want to make my heartbeat flow within Yours to soothe the harrowing spasm that You suffer. And my heartbeat in Yours swears loyalty and love to You, and repeats and swears thousands and thousands of times that I know You.

But your love is not yet calmed, and You try to look at Peter. At your loving glances, dripping with tears because of his denial, Peter is moved, and he cries and leaves. Having led him to safety, You calm Yourself, and in this way repair the offenses of the Popes and of the leaders of the Church, especially of those who expose themselves to occasions.

Meanwhile, your enemies continue to accuse You; and in seeing that You do not answer to their accusations, Caiphas says to You: "I beseech You, for the sake of the living God, tell me - are You really the true Son of God?"

And You, my Love, having the word of truth always on your lips, with supreme Majesty, and with sonorous and gentle voice, such that all are struck, and the very demons plunge themselves into the abyss, answer: "You say so. Yes, I am the true Son of God, and one day I will descend on the clouds of Heaven to judge all nations."

At your creative words, all remain silent - they shudder and feel frightened. But Caiphas, recovering after a few moments of fright, full of rage, more than a fierce animal, says to all: "What need do we have of more witnesses? He has already uttered a great blasphemy! What more are we waiting for to condemn him? He is already guilty to death!"

And to give more strength to his words, he tears his clothes with such rage and fury that all, as though one, hurl themselves at You, my Good; some punch your head, some tear your hair, some slap You, some spit on your Face, some trample upon You. The torments that they give You are so intense and so many that the earth trembles and the Heavens are shaken.

My Love and my Life, Jesus, as they torment You, my poor heart is lacerated by the pain. O please, allow me to leave your sorrowful Heart and face all these offenses in your place. Ah, if it were possible, I would like to snatch You from the hands of your enemies. But You do not want it, because the salvation of all requires it, and I am forced to resign myself. But, sweet Love of mine, let me tidy You up, fix your hair, remove the spit, dry your Blood, and enclose myself in your Heart, as I see that Caiphas, tired, wants to withdraw, delivering You into the hands of the soldiers.

Therefore, I bless You; and You, bless me and give me the kiss of your love. And I enclose myself in the furnace of your Divine Heart to sleep. I place my mouth on your Heart, so that in breathing, I may kiss You, and from the differences in your heartbeats, more or less suffering, I may sense whether You are suffering or resting. Therefore, making wings of my arms to keep You sheltered, I hug You, I cling tightly to your Heart, and I fall asleep.

## REFLECTIONS AND PRACTICES
## by St. Hannibal di Francia

Jesus, presented to Caiphas, is unjustly accused and subjected to unheard-of tortures. Questioned, He always says the truth.

And we - when the Lord allows that we be slandered and unjustly accused, do we look only for God, who knows our innocence; or do we rather beg esteem and honor from creatures? Does truth always arise on our lips? Are we averse to any trick and lie? Do we bear with patience the mockeries and the confusions that creatures give us? Are we ready to give our life for their salvation?

O my sweet Jesus, how different I am from you! Please, let my lips speak always the truth so as to wound the heart of those who listen to me, and lead everyone to You!

# Twelfth Hour

From 4 to 5 AM

## Jesus at the mercy of the soldiers

My most sweet Life, Jesus, while sleeping, clinging to your Heart, I often felt the pricks of the thorns which prick your Most Holy Heart. Wanting to wake up together with You, that You may have at least one who notices all of your pains and feels compassion for You, I cling more tightly to your Heart; and feeling your prickings more vividly, I wake up. But, what do I see? What do I hear? I would like to hide You in my heart to expose myself in your place, and receive upon myself pains so intense, insults and humiliations so incredible. But only your love could bear so many outrages. My most patient Jesus, what could You expect from people so inhuman?

I now see that they are making fun of You. They cover your Face with thick spit; the light of your beautiful eyes is covered by the spit; and You, pouring rivers of tears for our salvation, push that spit away from your eyes, and your enemies, with hearts incapable of seeing the light of your eyes, cover them with spit again. Others, becoming more brave in evil, open your most sweet mouth and fill it with disgusting spit, to the point that they themselves feel nausea. And since some of that spit flows away, revealing, in part, the majesty of your Face and your superhuman sweetness, they shudder and feel ashamed of themselves. In order to feel more free, they blindfold You with a miserable rag, to be able to hurl themselves,

94

unrestrained, at your adorable Person. And so they beat You up without pity; they drag You; they trample You under their feet; they repeat blows and slaps to your Face and over your head, scratching You, tearing your hair, and pushing You from one point to another.

Jesus, my Love, my heart cannot bear seeing You in the midst of so many pains. You want me to notice everything, but I feel I would rather cover my eyes so as not to see scenes so painful, which tear the heart from any chest. But my love for You forces me to look at what happens to You.

I see that You utter not a breath, that You say not a word to defend Yourself; that You are in the hands of these soldiers like a rag, and they can do with You whatever they want. And in seeing them jumping over You, I fear You may die under their feet. My Good and my All, the sorrow I feel for your pains is so great, that I would like to shout so loudly as to be heard up there in Heaven, and call the Father, the Holy Spirit and all the Angels; and here on earth, from one point to another, call sweet Mama first, and all the souls who love You, so that, forming a circle around You, we may prevent these insolent soldiers from drawing near You to insult You and torment You more. Together with You, we repair for all the night sins, especially those committed at night by sectarians, over your Sacramental Person, and for all the offenses of the souls who do not remain faithful in the night of trial.

But I see, my insulted Good, that the soldiers, tired and drunk, would like to rest, and my poor heart, oppressed and lacerated by your so many pains, does not want to remain alone with You – it feels the need of another company. O please, my sweet Mama, be my inseparable company; let us embrace Jesus together, in order to console Him! O Jesus, together with Mama, I kiss You and I bless You; and with Her, I will have the sleep of love upon your adorable Heart.

## REFLECTIONS AND PRACTICES
## by St. Hannibal di Francia

In this hour Jesus is in the midst of the soldiers with imperturbability and iron constancy. God as He is, He suffers all the strains which the soldiers inflict upon Him, and looks at them with so much love that He seems to invite them to give Him more pains. And we - are we constant during repeated sufferings, or do we lament, get irritated and lose peace; that peace of the heart which is necessary to allow Jesus to find a happy dwelling within us?

Firmness is that virtue which makes us know whether God really reigns in us. If ours is true virtue, we will be firm in trial, with a firmness which is not inconstant, but always equal to itself. The more we become firm in good, in suffering, in working, the more we enlarge the field around us, in which Jesus will expand His graces. Therefore, if we are inconstant, our field will be small, and Jesus will have little or no space. But if we are firm and constant, as Jesus finds a very extensive field, He will find in us His shelf and support, and the place in which to extend His graces.

If we want our beloved Jesus to rest in us, let us surround Him with His own firmness, with which He operated for the salvation of our souls. Being sheltered, He will remain in our heart in sweet rest. Jesus looked with love at those who mistreated Him. Do we look at those who offend us with the same love? Is the love we show to them so great as to be a voice for their hearts - so powerful as to convert them to Jesus?

My Jesus, boundless Love, give me this love and let each pain of mine call souls to You.

## Thirteenth Hour

From 5 to 6 AM

### Jesus in prison

My Prisoner Jesus, I have awakened and I do not find You. My heart beats very strongly; it fidgets with love. Tell me, where are You? My Angel, bring me to the house of Caiphas. But I go round and round, I search everywhere, and I do not find You. My Love, hurry, with your hands move the chains with which You keep my heart bound to Yours, and draw me to You, that I may take flight and come to throw myself into your arms. And You, Jesus, my Love, wounded by my voice and wanting my company, draw me toward You; and I see that they have put You in prison. My heart exults with joy in finding You, but I feel it wounded with sorrow in seeing the state to which they have reduced You.

I see You with your hands tied behind You to a column, and with your feet bound and gripped. I see your most holy Face bruised, swollen and bleeding from the horrible slaps received. Your most pure eyes are blackened; your pupils are tired and sad from the vigil; your hair is all disarranged; your Most Holy Person is all beaten up, and You cannot even help Yourself and clean Yourself, because You are bound.

And I, O my Jesus, with a sob of crying, clinging to your feet, say: 'Alas, how You have been reduced, O Jesus!'

And Jesus, looking at me, answers: "Come, oh my child, and be attentive to everything you see Me doing, in order to do it together with Me, that I may continue my Life in you."

To my amazement, I now see that instead of occupying Yourself with your pains, with an indescribable love, You think about glorifying the Father, to compensate Him for all that we owe; and You call all souls around You, to take all of their evils upon Yourself and give to them all goods. And since the day is dawning, I hear your most sweet voice say: "Holy Father, I give You thanks for all I have suffered and for all that is left for Me to suffer. And just as this dawn calls the day and the day makes the sun rise, so may the dawn of Grace arise in all hearts; and as daylight rises, may I, Divine Sun, rise in all hearts and reign over all. Do you see these souls, O Father? I want to answer You for all of them, for their thoughts, words, works and steps - at the cost of blood and death."

My Jesus, Love with no boundaries, I unite myself to You, and I too thank You for all that You have made me suffer, and for all that is left for me to suffer. And I pray You to make the dawn of Grace arise within all hearts, so that You, Divine Sun, may rise again in all hearts and reign over them.

But I also see, my sweet Jesus, that You repair for all the very first thoughts, affections and words, which, at the rising of the day, are not offered to You to honor You; and that You call to Yourself, as though in custody, the thoughts, the affections and the words of the creatures, in order to repair for them and give to the Father the glory they owe Him.

My Jesus, Divine Master, since we have one hour free in this prison and we are alone, not only do I want to do what You are doing, but I want to clean You, fix your hair, and fuse myself completely in You. So I draw near your most sacred head, and in rearranging your hair, I want to repair for so many minds, distraught and full of earth, which have not one thought for You. Fusing myself in your mind, I want to reunite all the thoughts of creatures within You and fuse them in your thoughts, in order to find sufficient reparation for all evil thoughts, and for so many suffocated enlightenments and inspirations. I would like to make all thoughts one with Yours, to give You true reparation and perfect glory.

My afflicted Jesus, I kiss your eyes, sad and filled with tears. Having your hands bound to the column, You cannot dry them, nor remove the spit with which they smeared You. And since the position in which they bound You is excruciating, You cannot close your tired eyes to take rest. My Love, how gladly would I offer You my arms as bed, to give You rest. I want to dry your eyes, ask for your forgiveness, and repair for all the times we have not had the aim of pleasing You, and of looking at You to see what You wanted from us, what we were supposed to do, and where You wanted us to go. I want to fuse my eyes in Yours, and also those of all creatures, to be able to repair with your own eyes for all the evil we have done with our sight.

My compassionate Jesus, I kiss your most holy ears, tired from the insults of the whole night, and much more so from the echo of all the offenses of creatures which resounds in your hearing. I ask for your forgiveness, and I repair for all the times You have called us and we have been deaf, or we have pretended not to hear You; and You, my weary Good, have repeated your calls – but in vain! I want to fuse my hearing in Yours, and also that of all creatures, to make a continuous and complete reparation.

Enamored Jesus, I adore and kiss your most holy Face, all bruised by the slapping. I ask for forgiveness and I repair for all the times You have called us to offer reparation, and we, uniting to your enemies, have given You slaps and spit. My Jesus, I want to fuse my face in Yours, to restore your natural beauty, giving You full reparation for all the contempt given to your adorable Majesty.

My embittered Good, I kiss your most sweet mouth, hurt by blows and parched by love. I want to fuse my tongue in Yours, and also the tongues of all creatures, in order to repair with your own tongue for all sins and evil discourses. And I want, my thirsty Jesus, to unite all voices into one with Yours, so that, when we are about to offend You, as your voice flows in those of all creatures, it may suffocate the voices of sin and turn them into voices of praise and of love.

Chained Jesus, I kiss your neck, oppressed by heavy chains and by ropes, which, going from your chest to the back of your shoulders and passing through your arms, keep You bound, very tightly, to the column. Your hands are already swollen and blackened from the tightness of

101

the knots, and they spurt blood from several points. O please, allow me to release You, my bound Jesus; and if You love to be bound, allow me to bind You with the chains of love, which, being sweet, instead of making You suffer, will soothe You. And as I release You, I want to fuse myself in your neck, in your chest, in your shoulders, in your hands, in your feet, to be able to repair together with You for all attachments, and therefore give to all the chains of your love; to be able to repair with You for all the coldness, and so fill the breasts of all creatures with your fire, as I see that You have so much of it, that You are unable to contain it; and to be able to repair with You for all illicit pleasures and for love of comforts, to give to everyone the spirit of sacrifice and love of suffering.

And I want to fuse myself in your hands to repair for all the evil works, for the good done badly and with presumptuousness, and give to all the fragrance of your works. I want to fuse myself in your feet, to block all the steps of creatures, and so repair for them and give your steps to all, to make them walk in a saintly way.

Finally, my sweet Life, as I fuse myself in your Heart, allow me to enclose all the affections, heartbeats and desires, to repair for them together with You, and to give to everyone your affections, heartbeats and desires, so that no one may ever again offend You.

But I hear the noise of the creaking of the key: your enemies are now coming to take You out of prison. And I tremble, Jesus; I feel my blood running cold. You will again be in the hands of your enemies. What will happen to You? I seem also to hear the creaking of the keys of the tabernacles. How many desecrating hands come to open them, and maybe to make You descend into sacrilegious hearts? Into how many unworthy hands You are forced to find Yourself! My prisoner Jesus, I want to be in all of your prisons of love, to be spectator when your ministers release You, and to keep You company and repair for the offenses You may receive.

I see that your enemies are near, while You greet the rising sun on the last of your days. As they untie You, in seeing that You are all majesty and that You look at them with so much love, in return they unload onto your Face slaps so violent as to make It turn red with your most precious Blood.

Jesus, my Love, before leaving the prison, in my sorrow I ask You to bless me, in order to receive the strength to follow You along the rest of your Passion.

## REFLECTIONS AND PRACTICES
### by St. Hannibal di Francia

In prison, tied to a pillar and immobilized, Jesus is smeared with spittle and mud. He looks for our souls to keep Him company. And we - are we happy to be alone with Jesus, or do we look for the company of creatures? Is Jesus alone our only breath and our only heartbeat?

In order to make us become like Him, loving Jesus binds our souls with aridity, with oppressions, with sufferings, and with any other kind of mortification. Are we happy to

103

be bound by Jesus in that prison in which His love places us - that is, obscurity, oppressions and the like?

Jesus is in prison. Do we feel the firmness and the promptness to imprison ourselves in Jesus for love of Him? Afflicted Jesus longed for our souls in order to be untied and sustained in the painful position in which He found Himself. Do we long for Jesus alone to come and keep us company, to free us from the chains of every passion, and to bind us with the stronger chains of His Heart? Do we place our pains as cortege around suffering Jesus in order to remove from Him the spit and the mud which sinners send to Him? Jesus prays in prison. Is our prayer constant with Jesus?

My chained Jesus, You made Yourself a prisoner for love of me, and I pray You to imprison my mind, my tongue, my heart and all of myself within You, that I may have no freedom, and You may have absolute lordship over me.

# Fourteenth Hour

From 6 to 7 AM

## Jesus before Caiphas again, who confirms

## His condemnation to death and sends Him to Pilate

My sorrowful Jesus, You are now out of the prison; You are so exhausted that You stagger at each step. I want to place myself at your side in order to sustain You, when I see that You are about to fall.

But I see that the soldiers take You before Caiphas; and You, O my Jesus, reappear in their midst like a Sun, and even though disfigured, You spread light everywhere. I now see that Caiphas is overjoyed in seeing You reduced so badly. At the reflections of your Light, he becomes more blinded, and in his fury, he asks You again: "So, are You really the true Son of God?"

And You, my Love, with supreme majesty, with the grace of your word, and with your usual sweet and moving tone, such as to enrapture the hearts, answer: "Yes, I am the true Son of God."

And your enemies, though feeling all the power of your word within themselves, suffocating everything, wanting to know nothing else – in one voice, cry out: "He is guilty to death. He is guilty to death!"

Caiphas confirms the sentence to death, and sends You to Pilate. And You, my condemned Jesus, accept this sentence with so much love and resignation, as to almost snatch it from the iniquitous Pontiff. You repair for all the sins committed deliberately and with all malice, and for those who, instead of afflicting themselves because of evil, rejoice and exult over sin itself, and this leads them to blindness and to suffocating any enlightenment and grace. My Life, Jesus, your reparations and prayers echo in my heart, and I repair and pray together with You.

My sweet Love, I see that, having lost any bit of esteem for You, seeing You sentenced to death, the soldiers grab You, add ropes and chains, and bind You so tightly as to almost prevent any movement of your Divine Person; and pushing You and dragging You, they put You out of the palace of Caiphas.

Crowds of people await You – but no one to defend You. And You, my Divine Sun, come out into their midst, wanting to envelop everyone with your Light. As You move the first steps, wanting to enclose all the steps of creatures within yours, You pray and repair for those who move the first steps to operate with evil purposes – some to take revenge, some to steal, some to betray, some to kill, and more. Oh, how all these sins wound your Heart! And in order to prevent so much evil, You pray, You repair, and You offer all of Yourself.

But, as I follow You, I see that at the moment of descending from the palace of Caiphas, You, my Sun, Jesus, meet beautiful Mary, our sweet Mama. Your gazes meet and wound each other; and even though You feel relieved in seeing each other, yet new sorrows arise: for You, in seeing the beautiful Mama pierced, pale and wrapped in mourning; and for dear Mama, in seeing You, Divine Sun, eclipsed and covered with so much opprobrium - crying and wrapped in Blood. But You cannot enjoy the exchange of your gazes for too long, and with the sorrow of being unable to say even a word to each other, your Hearts say everything; and one fused within the other, You stop looking at each other, because the soldiers are pushing You.

So, trampled upon and dragged, You arrive at Pilate. My Jesus, I unite myself to your pierced Mama in following You, to fuse myself in You together with Her. And You, give me your gaze of love, and bless me.

## REFLECTIONS AND PRACTICES
## by St. Hannibal di Francia

Jesus goes out to the light of the day and is brought before Caiphas. With firmness He confirms that He is the Son of God.

When we go out, do we let ourselves be directed by Jesus? Is our composure an example for others, and our steps like magnets which call souls around Jesus? The whole life of Jesus is a continuous cry for souls. If we conform to His Will - that is, if our feet call souls as they walk, if our heartbeats, echoing the divine heartbeats, harmonize with them and ask for souls, and so on with all the rest - as we operate in this way, we will form the very Humanity of Jesus within ourselves. Therefore, every additional cry for souls that we make, is an additional mark that we receive from our Jesus. Is our life always the same, or do we change it for the worse, depending on the encounters that we have?

My Jesus, sanctity which has no equal, guide me, and let also my outward appearance manifest all your divine life.

# Fifteenth Hour

From 7 to 8 AM

## Jesus before Pilate. Pilate sends Him to Herod

My bound Good, Jesus, your enemies, together with the priests, present You to Pilate; and faking sanctity and scrupulousness, because they have to celebrate the Passover, they remain outside the lobby. And You, my Love, seeing the depth of their malice, repair for all the hypocrisies of the religious body. I too repair together with You. But while You occupy Yourself with their good, they begin to accuse You before Pilate, vomiting all the poison they have against You.

Showing himself unsatisfied with the accusations they make against You, Pilate calls You aside, to be able to condemn You with reason, and, alone, he examines You and asks You: "Are you the king of the Jews?"

And You, Jesus, my true King, answer: "My Kingdom is not of this world; otherwise, thousands of legions of Angels would defend Me."

And Pilate, moved by the sweetness and the dignity of your words, surprised, says to You: "So, you are a king?"

And You: "You say it - I am, and I have come into the world to teach the Truth."

Without wanting to know anything else, convinced of your innocence, Pilate goes out to the lobby and says: "I find no guilt in this man."

Enraged, the Jews accuse You of many other things, and You remain silent; You do not defend Yourself. You repair for the weaknesses of the judges, when they are faced by the arrogant; You repair for their injustices, and You pray for the innocent, oppressed and abandoned.

Then, seeing the fury of your enemies, Pilate sends You to Herod, to get rid of You.

## Jesus before Herod

My Divine King, I want to repeat your prayers and reparations, as I accompany You to Herod.

I see that your enemies, enraged, would want to devour You, and they lead You among insults, mockeries and derisions. So, they make You arrive before Herod, who, swelling up, asks You many questions. You do not answer him and do not even look at him. And Herod, irritated because he does not see his curiosity satisfied, and feeling humiliated by your long silence, declares to all that You are crazy and mindless, and he orders that You be treated as such. And to mock You, he has You clothed with a white garment, and he delivers You into the hands of the soldiers, that they may do with You the worst they can.

My innocent Jesus, no one finds guilt in You – only the Jews, because their faked religiosity does not deserve that the light of Truth may shine in their minds.

My Jesus, infinite Wisdom, how much it costs You being declared insane! Abusing You, the soldiers cast You to the ground, trample You, smear You with spit, despise You, beat You with rods, and the blows are so many that You feel You are dying. The pains, the ignominies, the humiliations they inflict on You, are so great and so many that the Angels weep, and cover their faces with their wings in order not to see them.

My crazy Jesus, I too want to call You crazy – but crazy with love. And your folly of love is such that, instead of becoming upset, You pray and repair for the ambitions of the kings and of the leaders, who aspire to kingdoms for the ruin of the peoples; for the many slaughters they cause, and the so much blood they cause to be shed for their whims; for the sins committed in the courts, in the palaces, and in the militia.

My Jesus, how tender it is to see You pray and repair in the midst of so many outrages! Your voice resounds in my heart, and I follow whatever You do. And now, let me place myself at your side, share in your pains, and console You with my love. Driving the enemies away from You, I take You in my arms to refresh You, and to kiss your forehead.

My sweet Love, I see that they give You no peace – Herod sends You to Pilate. If coming was painful, going back will be more tragic, because I see that the Jews are more furious than before, and they are determined to make You die at any cost.

Therefore, before You leave the palace of Herod, I want to kiss You to prove my love to You, in the midst of so many pains. And You, strengthen me with your kiss and with your blessing, that I may follow You before Pilate.

## REFLECTIONS AND PRACTICES
## by St. Hannibal di Francia

Presented to Pilate, in the midst of many insults and scorns, Jesus is always sweet; He disdains no one, and tries to make the light of truth shine in everyone. Do we feel the same with everyone? Do we try to conquer our natural evil if someone does not sympathize with us? In dealing with creatures, do we always try to make Jesus known, and to make the light of truth shine in them?

O Jesus, sweet Life of mine, place your word on my lips, and let me always speak with your tongue.

Clothed as a madman before Herod, Jesus remains silent, suffering unheard-of pains. And we - when we are slandered, mocked, insulted or derided, do we think that the Lord wants to give us a divine likeness? In the pains, in the scorns, and in all that our poor heart may feel, do we think that it is Jesus who gives us sorrow with His touch, who transforms us into Himself with His touch, and gives us His likeness? And as suffering returns to us, do we think that Jesus, in looking at us, is not satisfied with us, and therefore gives us another squeeze in order to render us completely like Him? Following the example of Jesus, can we say that we have dominion over ourselves; and that, in adversities, we prefer to remain silent instead of answering? Do we ever let ourselves be overcome by curiosity? In every pain that we may suffer, we must place the intention that it be a life which we give to Jesus in order to plead for souls. Placing souls in the Will of God, our pain becomes a circle, in which we enclose God and the souls in order to join them to Jesus.

My Love and my All, You alone, take dominion over this heart of mine and keep it in your hands, so that in any encounter I may copy within me your infinite patience.

# Sixteenth Hour

From 8 to 9 AM

## Jesus is brought back to Pilate and placed after Barabbas.

## Jesus is scourged

My tormented Jesus, my poor heart follows You in the midst of anxieties and pains, and in seeing You clothed as a madman, knowing who You are - Infinite Wisdom, who gives reason to all - I become delirious, and I say: "How can it be! Jesus – insane? Jesus – a criminal? And as if it was not enough, You will now be placed after Barabbas!"

My Jesus, Sanctity which has no equal, You are already before Pilate, once again. In seeing You reduced so badly, clothed as a madman, that not even Herod has condemned You, he becomes more indignant against the Jews, and is even more convinced of your innocence, and that he should not condemn You. But, still, wanting to give some satisfaction to the Jews, almost to dampen their hatred, their fury, their rage, and their ardent thirst for your Blood, proposes You, with Barabbas, for their choice. But the Jews cry out: "We do not want Jesus free, but Barabbas!"

And Pilate, not knowing what to do to calm them, condemns You to the scourging.

My Jesus, placed last - my heart breaks in seeing that, while the Jews occupy themselves with You to make You die, You, instead, recollected within Yourself, think about giving Life to all. And as I prick up my ear, I hear You say: "Holy Father, look at your Son, clothed as a madman. May this repair before You for the madness of many creatures fallen into sin. May this white garment be like a defense before You, for many souls who clothe themselves with the dismal garment of sin. Do You see, O Father, their hatred, their fury, their rage against Me, which almost makes them lose the light of reason, for thirst for my Blood? And I want to repair for all of the hatreds, the revenges, the anger, the murders, and impetrate the light of reason for all.

Look at Me again, my Father; can there be greater insult? They have placed Me after the greatest criminal. And I want to repair for all the misplacements they do. Ah, the whole world is full of misplacements: some place Us after a vile interest, some after honors, some after vanities, some after pleasures, some after their own attachments, some after dignities, some after gluttonies, and even after sin. All creatures unanimously place Us after even a tiny little trifle. And I am ready to accept being placed after Barabbas, in order to repair for the misplacements the creatures make with Us."

My Jesus, I feel I am dying with sorrow and confusion in seeing your great love in the midst of so many pains, and the heroism of your virtues in the midst of so many pains and insults. Your words and reparations resound in my poor heart like many wounds, and in my torment, I repeat your prayers and your reparations. Not even for one instant do I want to detach myself from You, otherwise many of the things You do would escape me. And now, what do I see? The soldiers take You to a pillar in order to scourge You. My Love, I follow You; and You, look at me with your loving gaze, and give me the strength to be present at your painful massacre.

## Jesus is scourged

My most pure Jesus, You are now near the pillar. Enraged, the soldiers untie You in order to bind You to it. But this is not enough – they strip You of your garments to make a cruel massacre of your Most Holy Body. My Love, my Life, I feel faint for the sorrow of seeing You naked. You tremble from head to foot, and your most holy Face blushes with virginal modesty. Your confusion, your exhaustion, are such that, unable to keep standing, You are about to fall at the foot of the pillar; but the soldiers sustain You – not to help You, but to bind You; and they do not let You fall.

They now take the ropes and bind your arms so tightly, that they swell immediately, and blood spurts from the ends of your fingers. Then, from the ring of the pillar, they make ropes and chains pass around your Most Holy Person, down to your feet; and to be able to freely hurl themselves at You, they bind You to the pillar so tightly that You cannot make one movement.

My stripped Jesus, allow me to pour myself out, otherwise I cannot go on seeing You suffer so much. How can this be? You, who clothe all created things – the sun with light, the heavens with stars, the plants with leaves, the birds with feathers – You, stripped!? What daring! But my loving Jesus, through the light He sends forth from His eyes, tells me: "Be silent, O child - it was necessary that I be stripped, in order to repair for many who strip themselves of every modesty, of purity and of innocence; who strip themselves of every good and virtue, and of my Grace, clothing themselves with every brutality, and living like brutes. With my virginal blush I wanted to repair for so many dishonesties, luxuries and brutal pleasures. Therefore, be attentive to everything I do; pray and repair with Me, and calm yourself."

Scourged Jesus, your love moves from one excess to another. I see that the executioners take the ropes, and beat You without pity, to the point of bruising all of your Most Holy Body. Their fierceness, their fury in beating You is such that they are already tired. But two more take their place; they take thorny rods, and they beat You so much that, soon, rivers of Blood begin to pour from your Most Holy Body. Then they lash it all over, forming furrows, and filling it with wounds. But this is not all; two more take their turn, and with hooked iron chains, they continue the excruciating massacre. At the first blows, that flesh, beaten and wounded, rips open even more, and falls to the ground, torn into pieces. The bones are uncovered, the Blood pours down – so much, as to form a pool of Blood around the pillar.

My Jesus, my stripped Love, while You are under this storm of blows, I cling to your feet, to take part in your pains and be covered completely by your most precious

Blood. But each blow You receive is a wound to my heart; more so, since in pricking up my ears, I hear your moans. But they are not heard, because the storm of the blows deafens the air all around. And in those moans, You say: "All of you who love Me, come to learn the heroism of true love! Come to dampen in my Blood the thirst of your passions, your thirst for so many ambitions, for so many intoxications and pleasures, for so much sensuality! In this Blood of Mine you will find the remedy for all of your evils."

Your moans continue to say: "Look at Me, O Father, all wounded under this storm of blows. But this is not enough; I want to form so many wounds in my Body as to give enough rooms to all souls within the Heaven of my Humanity, in such a way as to form their salvation within Myself, and then let them pass into the Heaven of the Divinity. My Father, may each blow of these scourges repair before You for each kind of sin – one by one. And as they strike Me, let them justify those who commit them. May these blows strike the hearts of creatures, and speak to them about my love, to the point of forcing them to surrender to Me."

And as You say this, your love is so great, though great is the pain, that You almost incite the executioners to beat You more. My Jesus, stripped of your own flesh, your love crushes me – I feel I am going mad. Your love is not tired, while the executioners are exhausted and cannot continue your painful massacre.

They now cut the ropes, and You, almost dead, fall into your own Blood. And in seeing the shreds of your flesh, You feel like dying of grief, because in those detached pieces of flesh You see the reprobate souls. And your sorrow is such, that You gasp in your own Blood.

My Jesus, allow me to take You in my arms, in order to refresh You a little with my love. I kiss You, and with my kiss, I enclose all souls in You, so no one will be lost; and You - bless me.

## REFLECTIONS AND PRACTICES
### by St. Hannibal di Francia

From 8 to 9 Jesus is stripped naked and subjected to cruel scourging. And we - are we stripped of everything? Jesus is tied to the pillar. Do we let ourselves be bound by love? Jesus is tied to the pillar, while we add our own ropes, with our sins and attachments, and sometimes even with things which are indifferent or good in themselves, not being satisfied with the ropes with which the Jews tied Him. In the meantime, with His pitying gaze Jesus calls us to untie Him. Don't we see that in that gaze there is also a reproach for us, since we too contributed to binding Him? In order to relieve afflicted Jesus, we must remove our chains first, to be able to arrive at removing the chains of other creatures. Many times these little chains of ours are nothing other than little attachments to our own will, to our self-love which is a little resentful; to our little vanities which, forming a braid, painfully bind loving Jesus.

Sometimes, taken by love for our poor soul, Jesus Himself wants to take these chains away from us, so that we may not repeat His painful binding. Ah, when we lament because we don't want to be bound alone with Jesus, we force Him, saddened, to withdraw from us.

While He suffers, our tormented Jesus repairs all the sins against modesty. And we - are we pure in the mind, in the gaze, in the words, in the affections, so as not to add more blows on that innocent Body? Are we always bound to Jesus, so as to be ready to defend Him, when creatures strike Him with their offenses?

My chained Jesus, may your chains be my own, so that I may always feel You in Me, and You may always feel me within You.

# Seventeenth Hour

From 9 to 10 AM

## Jesus is crowned with thorns. Presented to the people: "Ecce Homo!"
## Jesus is condemned to death

My Jesus, infinite Love, the more I look at You, the more I understand how much You suffer. You are already completely lacerated – there is not one point left whole in You. The executioners, enraged in seeing that, in so many pains, You look at them with so much love; and in seeing that your loving gaze, forming a sweet enchantment, almost like many voices, prays and supplicates for more pains and new pains - though inhuman, yet forced by your love, make You stand on your feet. Unable to stand Yourself, You fall again into your own Blood, and, irritated, with kicks and shoves, they make You reach the place where they will crown You with thorns.

My Love, if You do not sustain me with your gaze of love, I cannot go on seeing You suffer. I feel a shiver in my bones, my heart throbs, I feel I am dying. Jesus, Jesus – help me!

And my lovable Jesus says to me: "My child, courage, do not miss anything of what I suffered. Be attentive to my teachings. I have to redo man in everything. Sin has removed the crown from him, and has crowned him with opprobrium and with confusion; so he cannot stand before my Majesty. Sin has dishonored him, making him lose any right to honors and to glory. This is why I want to be crowned with thorns – to place the crown on man's forehead, and to return to him all rights to every honor and glory. Before my Father, my thorns will be reparations and voices of defense for many sins of thought, especially pride; and for each created mind they will be voices of light and supplication, that they may not offend Me. Therefore, unite yourself to Me, and pray and repair together with Me."

Crowned Jesus, your cruel enemies make You sit; they place a rag of purple on You, they take the crown of thorns, and with infernal fury, they put it on your adorable head. Then, by blow of rod, they make the thorns penetrate into your forehead, and some of them reach into your eyes, into your ears, into your skull, and even behind your neck. My Love, what torment, what unspeakable pains! How many cruel deaths You suffer!

Your Blood pours down upon your Face, in such a way that one can see nothing but blood. But under those thorns and that Blood, your most holy Face appears, radiant with sweetness, with peace, and with love. And the executioners, wanting to complete the tragedy, blindfold You, place a reed in your hand as scepter, and begin their mockeries. They hail You King of the Jews, they beat You on the crown, they slap You, and say to You: "Guess who hit You!"

And You remain silent – You answer by repairing for the ambition of those who aspire to kingdoms, to dignities, to honors, and for those who, finding themselves in positions of authority and behaving incorrectly, cause the ruin of the peoples and of their souls, which had been entrusted to them; and their evil examples push others toward evil and cause the loss of souls.

With this reed You hold in your hand, You repair for so many works - good, but empty of interior spirit and also done with evil intentions. In the insults and the blindfold, You repair for those who ridicule the holiest things, discrediting them and profaning them; You also repair for those who blindfold the sight of their intelligence in order not to see the light of Truth. With this blindfold, You impetrate that the blindfolds of passions, of riches and of pleasures may be removed from us.

My King Jesus, your enemies continue with their insults. The Blood which flows from your most holy head is so much, that reaching your mouth, It prevents You from letting me hear clearly your most sweet voice, so I cannot do what You do. Therefore I come into your arms; I want to sustain your pierced and suffering head, and I want to place my head under those thorns in order to feel their pricks.

But as I say this, my Jesus calls me with His loving gaze, and quickly I embrace His Heart, and I try to sustain His head. Oh, how beautiful it is to be with Jesus, even in the midst of a thousand torments! And He says to me: "My child, these thorns say that I want to be constituted King of each heart; to Me belongs every dominion. Take these thorns and prick your heart; let everything that does not belong to Me come out, and then leave one thorn inside, as the seal that I am your King, and to prevent any other thing from entering into you. Then, go through every heart, and pricking them, let all the fumes of pride and the rottenness which they contain come out, and constitute Me King of all."

My Love, my heart breaks in leaving You; therefore I pray You to deafen my ears with your thorns, that I may hear only your voice; cover my eyes with your thorns, that I may look at You alone; fill my mouth with your thorns, that my tongue be mute to everything that may offend You, and be free to praise You and bless You in everything. O my King Jesus, surround me with thorns, that they may hold me in custody, defend me, and keep me all intent on You. And now I want to dry your Blood and kiss You, because I see that your enemies take You to Pilate, who will condemn You to death. My Love, help me to follow your Sorrowful Way, and bless me.

**Jesus once again before Pilate, who shows Him to the people.**

My crowned Jesus, wounded by your love and transfixed by your pains, my poor heart cannot live without You, so I search for You, and I find You before Pilate, once again.

But, what a moving scene! The Heavens are horrified, and hell trembles with fear and rage! Life of my heart, my gaze cannot bear the sight of You, without feeling itself dying. But the enrapturing power of your love forces me to look at You, that I may comprehend your pains well; and I contemplate You, amid tears and sighs.

My Jesus, You are naked, but still, You clothe Yourself – I see You are clothed with blood, your flesh torn, your

124

bones uncovered, your most holy Face unrecognizable. The thorns stuck in your most holy head reach into your eyes – into your Face, and I see nothing but blood which, pouring down to the ground, forms a bloody torrent behind your feet.

My Jesus, I can no longer recognize You because of the way You have been reduced! Your state has reached the most profound excesses of humiliations and spasms! Ah, I can no longer bear the sight of You, so sorrowful – I feel I am dying. I would want to snatch You from the presence of Pilate, to enclose You in my heart and give You rest. I would want to heal your wounds with my love, and flood the whole world with your Blood, to enclose all souls in it and conduct them to You, as the conquest of your pains!

And You, O patient Jesus, seem to look at me with difficulty through the thorns, and You say to me: "My child, come into these bound arms of mine, place your head on my breast, and you will see pains more intense and bitter, because what you see on the outside of my Humanity is nothing but the outpouring of my interior pains. Pay attention to the beats of my Heart, and you will hear that I repair for the injustices of those who command, for the oppressions against the poor and the innocents subordinated to kings, for the pride of those who, in order to preserve dignities, positions, riches, do not hesitate to break any law and to harm their neighbor, closing their eyes to the light of truth. With these thorns I want to shatter the spirit of pride of their lordships; and with the holes which they form in my head, I want to open my way into their minds, in order to reorder all things in them, according to the light of truth. By remaining so humiliated before this unjust judge, I want to make everyone understand that only virtue is that which constitutes man king of himself; and I teach to those who command, that virtue alone, united to upright knowledge, is worthy and capable of governing and ruling others, while all other dignities, without virtue, are dangerous and deplorable things. My child, echo my reparations, and continue to be attentive to my pains."

My Love, I see that in seeing You reduced so badly, Pilate shudders, and deeply impressed, exclaims: "How can there be so much cruelty in human breasts? Ah, this was not my will in condemning Him to the scourging!" And wanting to free You from the hands of the enemies - in order to find more convenient reasons, all humbled, removing his gaze from You because he cannot sustain your sight, too painful - he questions You again: "But, tell me, what have you done? Your people gave you into my hands – tell me, are you a king? What is your kingdom?"

At the storming questions of Pilate, You, O my Jesus, do not answer, and recollected within Yourself, You think about saving my poor soul, at the cost of so many pains!

Since You do not answer, Pilate adds: "Do you not know that it is in my power to release you or to condemn you?" But You, O my Love, wanting to make the light of truth shine in the mind of Pilate, answer: "You would have no power over Me, if it did not come to you from above. However, those who gave Me into your hands, have committed a sin graver than yours."

Almost moved by the sweetness of your voice, irresolute as he is, with his heart in a tempest, thinking that the Jews would be more compassionate, Pilate decides to show You from the lobby, hoping that they may be moved to compassion in seeing You so tortured, so as to be able to release You.

Sorrowful Jesus, my heart faints in seeing You follow Pilate. You walk with difficulty, bent over, under that horrible crown of thorns. Your Blood marks your steps, and as You go out, You hear the tumultuous crowd anxiously awaiting your condemnation. Imposing silence, in order to call the attention of all and to be heard by all, Pilate, with repugnance, takes two hems of the purple which covers your chest and shoulders. He lifts it, so that all may see how You are reduced, and says in a loud voice: "Ecce homo! [Here is the man!] Look at him – he no longer has the features of a man. Observe his wounds – he can no longer be recognized. If he has done evil, he has already suffered enough - or rather, too much. I already regret having made him suffer so much; therefore, let us set him free."

Jesus, my Love, allow me to sustain You, because I see that, unable to stand under the weight of so many pains, You stagger. Ah, in this solemn moment, your destiny is decided. At the words of Pilate, all become silent – in Heaven, on earth, and in hell! And then, as though in one single voice, I hear the cry of all: "Crucify Him, crucify Him – we want Him dead at any cost!"

My Life, Jesus, I see You tremble. The cry of death descends into your Heart, and among these voices, You recognize the voice of your dear Father, which says: "My Son, I want You dead, and dead crucified!" Ah, You hear also your Mama who, though pierced and desolate, echoes your dear Father: "Son, I want You dead!" The Angels, the Saints, hell – everyone, in one voice cries out: "Crucify Him, crucify Him!" There is not one soul who wants You alive. And – ah, ah! to my deepest blush, sorrow and horror, I too feel forced to cry out, by an irresistible force: "Crucify Him!"

My Jesus, forgive me if I too, a miserable sinful soul, want You dead! But, I pray You to make me die together with You. In the meantime, O my tormented Jesus, moved by my sorrow, You seem to say to me: "My child, cling to my Heart, and take part in my pains and in my reparations. This moment is solemn: either my death or the death of all creatures must be decided. In this moment, two currents pour into my Heart. In one there are all the souls who, if they want Me dead, it is because they want to find life in Me; and so, by my acceptance of death for them, they are released from the eternal condemnation, and the doors of Heaven open to receive them. In the other current there are those who want Me dead out of hatred and as confirmation of their own condemnation; and my Heart is lacerated, and feels the death of each one of them, and the very pains of hell! Ah, my Heart cannot bear these bitter pains; I feel death at each heartbeat, at each breath, and I keep repeating: 'Why will so much blood be shed in vain? Why will my pains be useless for so many?' Ah, child, sustain Me, for I can take no more. Take part in my pains; may your life be a continuous offering for the salvation of souls, so as to soothe pains so excruciating for Me!"

My Heart, Jesus, your pains are mine, and I echo your reparations. But I see that Pilate is astonished, and he hastens to say: "How can this be? Should I crucify your king? I find no guilt in him to condemn him." And the Jews cry out, deafening the air: "We have no other king but Caesar, and if you do not condemn Him, you are not a friend of Caesar. Insane, insane - crucify Him, crucify Him!"

Not knowing what else to do, for fear of being deposed, Pilate has a bucket of water brought to him, and washing his hands, he says: "I am not responsible for the blood of this just one." And he condemns You to death. But the Jews cry out: "May His Blood fall upon us and upon our children!" And in seeing You condemned, they make feast, they clap their hands, they whistle and shout; while You, O Jesus, repair for those who, finding themselves in high positions, out of vain fear and in order not to lose their places, break the most sacred laws, not caring about the ruin of entire peoples, favoring the evil and condemning the innocent. You repair also for those who, after sin, provoke the divine wrath to punish them.

But while You repair for this, your Heart bleeds with sorrow in seeing your chosen people, struck by the malediction of Heaven, which they themselves, with full will, have wanted, sealing it with your Blood which they cursed! Ah, your Heart faints; allow me to sustain It in my hands, making your reparations and your pains my own. But your love pushes You higher and, impatient, You already look for the Cross!

My Life, I will follow You, but for now rest in my arms; then, we will reach Mount Calvary together. Therefore, remain in me, and bless me.

## REFLECTIONS AND PRACTICES
## by St. Hannibal di Francia


From 9 to 10, crowned with thorns, Jesus is mocked as king and subjected to unheard-of insults and pains. He repairs in a special way for the sins of pride. And we - do we avoid sentiments of pride? Do we attribute to God the good which we do? Do we consider ourselves inferior to others? Is our mind always empty of any other thought in order to give rise to grace? Many times we do not give rise to grace by keeping our mind filled with other thoughts. Then, since our mind is not completely filled with God, we ourselves cause the devil to bother us, and maybe we even foment temptations. When our mind is filled with God, as the devil approaches us, not finding the place toward which to direct his temptations, confused, he flees. In fact, holy thoughts have so much power against the devil that, as he is about to approach us, they wound him like many swords, and cast him away.


Therefore, we lament unfairly when our mind is bothered and tempted by the enemy. It is our poor surveillance that pushes our enemy to assault us. He is spying on our mind in order to find little gaps, and attack us. Then, instead of relieving Jesus with our holy thoughts and removing the thorns from Him, ungrateful, we push them into His head, making Him feel the pricking more sharply. In this way, grace remains frustrated, and cannot carry out the crafting of its holy inspirations in our mind.

Many times we do even worse. As we feel the weight of temptations, instead of bringing them to Jesus, making of them a bundle to be burned by the fire of His love, we worry, we become sad, and speculate on those very temptations. Therefore, not only does our mind remain occupied by evil thoughts, but all our poor being remains as though soaked with them; and so it would almost take a miracle from Jesus to free us. Jesus looks at us through those thorns and, calling us, He seems to say: "Ah, my child, you yourself do not want to cling to Me. If you had come soon to Me, I would have helped you to free yourself from the bothers which the enemy brought into your mind, and you would not have made Me sigh so much for your return. I asked for help from you in order to be freed from thorns so sharp; but I waited in vain, because you were occupied with the work that your enemy had given you. Oh! how much less tempted you would be, if you came soon into my arms. Fearing Me, and not you, the enemy would leave you immediately."

My Jesus, may your thorns seal my thoughts in your mind, and prevent the enemy from causing any sort of temptation. When Jesus makes Himself felt in our mind and in our heart, do we reciprocate His inspirations, or do we place them into oblivion? Jesus is mocked as king. And we - do we respect all the holy things? Do we use all the reverence which befits them, as if we were touching Jesus Christ Himself?

My crowned Jesus, let me feel your thorns, so that I may understand from their pricks how much You suffer, and I may constitute You as King of my whole self.

Showed from the lobby, Jesus is condemned to death by those people who had been loved and who had benefited so much from Him. Loving Jesus accepts death for us, in order to give us life. Are we ready to accept any pain to prevent Jesus from being offended and from suffering? Our pain must be accepted so as not to make Jesus suffer. Since He suffered infinitely in His Humanity, and since we have to continue His life on earth, we must reciprocate the pains of the Humanity of Jesus Christ with our own pains.

How do we compassionate the pains which Jesus suffers in seeing many souls being snatched from His Heart? Do we make His pains our own so as to relieve Him from all that He suffers? The Jews want Him crucified, so that He may die like a criminal, and that His name be erased from the face of the earth. Do we strive to let Jesus live on earth? With our acts, with our example, with our steps, we must put a divine mark in the world, so that Jesus may be recognized by all, and so that, through our works, His life may have a divine echo, heard from one end of the world to another. Are we ready to give our own life so that beloved Jesus may be relieved of all the offenses, or do we rather imitate the Jews, people so much favored - almost like our own souls, which are loved so much by Jesus - and shout like them, "Crucifigatur" (let Him be crucified)?

My condemned Jesus, may your condemnation be my own, which I accept for love of you. And in order to console You, I will pour myself continuously in You, to bring You into the hearts of all creatures, to make You known to all, and to give your life to all.

# The Eighteenth Hour

From 10 to 11 AM

## Jesus takes up the Cross and walks toward Calvary, where He is stripped

My Jesus, insatiable Love, I see that You give Yourself no peace, I feel your fidgets of love, your pains. Your Heart beats strongly; in every heartbeat I feel bursts, tortures, violences of love; and unable to contain the fire that devours You, You pant, moan, sigh, and in each moan I hear You say: "Cross!" Each drop of your Blood repeats: "Cross!" All your pains, through which You swim as though in an interminable sea, repeat among themselves: "Cross!" And You exclaim: "O Cross, beloved and longed for, You alone will save my children, and I concentrate in You all my love!"

## Second Crowning with Thorns.

Meanwhile, your enemies take You back into the Praetorium, and remove the purple mantle, wanting to clothe You again with your own garments. But, alas, how much pain! It would be sweeter for me to die than to see You suffer so much! The garment remains snagged to the crown, and they are unable to pull it off. So, with cruelty never before seen, they tear off everything together – garment and crown. At the cruel tearing, many thorns break, remaining stuck inside your most holy head. Blood pours down in torrents, and your pain is such that You moan. But the enemies, heedless of the tortures, clothe You with your own garment, and then put the crown back, pushing it violently upon your head. The thorns are driven into your eyes, into your ears – there is not one part of your most holy head that does not feel their piercing. Your pain is such that You stagger under those cruel hands, shivering from head to foot; You are about to die among atrocious spasms of pain, and with your languishing eyes, filled with blood, You look at Me, with difficulty, asking for help in so much pain!

My Jesus, King of Sorrows, let me sustain You and hold You tightly to my heart. I would want to take the fire that devours You to burn your enemies to ashes and rescue You; but You don't want it, because your yearnings for the Cross become more ardent, and You quickly want to immolate Yourself on It - also for your enemies! But as I hold You tightly to my heart, You, holding me tightly to Yours, tell me: "My child, let Me pour out my love; and together with Me, repair for those who do good and yet dishonor Me. These Jews clothe Me with my own garment in order to discredit Me even more before the people, to convince them that I am a criminal. In appearance, the action of clothing Me was good, but in its essence it was evil. Ah, how many do good works, administer Sacraments or attend them, with human, and even evil purposes. But good, done badly, leads to hardness; so I want to be crowned for the second time, with pains sharper than the first time, in order to shatter this hardness, and with my thorns, draw them to Myself. Ah, my child, this second crowning is much more painful. I feel my head swimming in the midst of thorns; at every movement I make, or blow they give to Me, I suffer many cruel deaths. In this way I repair for the malice of the offenses; I repair for those, who, in whatever interior state they find themselves, instead of thinking of their own sanctification, waste and reject my grace, giving Me back more piercing thorns; while I am forced to moan, to cry tears of blood, and to sigh for their salvation.

Ah, I do everything to love them, and the creatures do everything to offend Me! You, at least - do not leave Me alone in my pains and reparations."

**Jesus embraces the Cross.**

My tortured Good, with You I repair, with You I suffer. But I see that your enemies hurl You down the stairs; the people await You with fury and eagerness; they make You find the Cross ready, which You long for with many sighs. And You - with love You gaze on It, and with firm step You approach It and embrace It. But, before that, You kiss It, and as a shiver of joy runs through your Most Holy Humanity, with highest contentment You gaze on It again, measuring Its length and breadth. In It, already, You establish the portion for each creature. You dower them all, enough to bind them to the Divinity with a bond of marriage, and make them heirs of the Kingdom of Heaven. Then, unable to contain the love with which You love them, You kiss the Cross again, and say: "Adored Cross, finally I embrace you. You were the longing of my Heart, the martyrdom of my love. But you, O Cross, have delayed until now, while my steps were always toward you. Holy Cross, you were the goal of my desires, the purpose of my existence down here. In you I concentrate my whole being, in you I place all my children, and you will be their life, their light, defense, custody and strength. You will assist them in everything, and will bring them gloriously to Me in Heaven. Oh Cross, Pulpit of Wisdom, you alone will teach true sanctity; you alone will form the heroes, the athletes, the martyrs, the Saints. Beautiful Cross, you are my Throne, and since I have to leave the earth, you will remain in my place. To you I give all souls as dowry – keep them, save them; I entrust them to you!"

In saying this, eager, You let It be placed upon your most holy shoulders. Ah, my Jesus, the Cross is too light for your love, but the weight of our sins unites to that of the Cross - enormous and immense, as the expanse of the Heavens. And You, my wearied Good, You feel crushed under the weight of so many sins. Your soul is horrified at their sight, and feels the pain of each sin. Your Sanctity remains shaken before so much ugliness, and as the Cross weighs upon your shoulders, You stagger, You pant, and a mortal sweat creeps through your Most Holy Humanity. O please, my Love, I don't have the heart to leave You alone - I want to share the weight of the cross with You; and to relieve You from the weight of sins, I cling to your feet. I want to give You, in the name of all creatures, love for those who do not love You, praises for those who despise You, blessings, thanksgivings, obedience on behalf of all. I promise that in any offense You receive, I intend to offer You all of myself in reparation, to do the acts opposite to the offenses the creatures give You, and to console You with my kisses and continuous acts of love. But I see that I am too miserable; I need You to be able to really repair You. Therefore I unite myself to your Most Holy Humanity, and together with You I unite my thoughts to yours in order to repair for the evil thoughts – mine, and of all; my eyes to yours, to repair for the evil

136

glances; my mouth to yours, to repair for the blasphemies and the evil discourses; my heart to yours, to repair for the evil tendencies, desires and affections. In a word, I want to repair everything that your Most Holy Humanity repairs, uniting myself to the immensity of your Love for all, and to the immense good You do to all. But I am not yet content. I want to unite myself to your Divinity, and I dissolve my nothingness in It, and in this way I give You everything. I give You your Love to quench your bitternesses; I give You your Heart to relieve You from our coldness, lack of correspondence, ingratitude, and the little love of the creatures. I give You your Harmonies to cheer your hearing from the deafening blasphemies it receives. I give You your Beauty to relieve You from the ugliness of our souls, when we muddy ourselves in sin. I give You your Purity to relieve You from the lack of righteous intention, and from the mud and rot You see in many souls. I give You your Immensity to relieve You from the voluntary constraints into which souls put themselves. I give You your Ardor to burn all sins and all hearts, so that all may love You, and no one may offend You, ever again. In sum, I give You all that You are, to give You infinite satisfaction, eternal, immense and infinite love.

**The Painful Way to Calvary.**

My most patient Jesus, I see You take the first steps under the enormous weight of the Cross. I unite my steps to yours, and when You, weak, bled dry and staggering, are about to fall, I will be at your side to sustain You; I will place my shoulders beneath It, so as to share Its weight with You. Do not disdain me, but accept me as your faithful companion. Oh Jesus, You look at me, and I see that You repair for those who do not carry their crosses with resignation, but rather, they swear, get irritated, commit suicide, and commit murders. And for all You impetrate love and resignation to their crosses. But your pain is such that You feel crushed under the Cross. You have taken only the first steps, and You already fall under It. As You fall, You knock against the stones; the thorns are driven more into your head, while all your wounds are embittered, and pour out new Blood. And since You do not have the strength to get up, your enemies, irritated, try to make You stand with kicks and shoves.

My fallen Love, let me help You to stand, let me kiss You, dry your Blood, and repair together with You for those who sin out of ignorance, fragility and weakness. I pray You to give help to these souls.

My Life, Jesus, making You suffer unheard-of spasms, your enemies have managed to put You on your feet, and as You walk, staggering, I hear your panting breath. Your Heart beats more strongly and new pains pierce It intensely. You shake your head in order to clear your eyes from the blood that fills them, and You gaze anxiously. Ah, my Jesus, I understood everything - your Mama, who is searching for You like a moaning dove, wants to tell You one last word, and receive your last gaze; and You feel Her pains, Her heart lacerated in Yours, moved and wounded by Her love and by Yours. You see Her pushing Her way through the crowd, wanting at any cost to see You, to hug You, to give You the last good-bye. But You are more transfixed in seeing Her mortal paleness, and all of your pains reproduced in Her by force of love. If She lives, it is only by a miracle of your Omnipotence. You move your steps toward hers, but You can hardly exchange a glance!

Oh, pang of your two Hearts! The soldiers notice it, and with blows and shoving prevent Mama and Son from exchanging the last good-bye. The torment of both is such that your Mama remains petrified by the pain, and is about to die. Faithful John and the pious women sustain Her, while You fall again under the Cross. Then, your sorrowful Mama does with Her soul that which She cannot do with Her Body, because She is prevented: She enters into You, makes the Will of the Eternal One Her own, and associating Herself in all your pains, performs the office of your Mother, kisses You, repairs You, soothes You, and pours the balm of Her sorrowful love into all your wounds!

My suffering Jesus, I too unite with the pierced Mama. I make all your pains, and every drop of your Blood my own; in each wound I want to act as a mama for You, and together with Her, and with You, I repair for all the dangerous encounters, and for those who expose themselves to occasions of sin, or, forced by necessity to be exposed, remain entangled in sin.

Meanwhile, You moan, fallen under the Cross. The soldiers fear that You may die under the weight of so many martyrdoms, and from the shedding of so much Blood. In spite of this, by lashes and kicks, with difficulty, they manage to put You on your feet again. And You repair for repeated falls into sin, for mortal sins committed by every class of people, and You pray for obstinate sinners, shedding tears of blood for their conversion.

My Love, overcome with pain, while I follow You in these reparations, I see You stagger under the enormous weight of the Cross. You are shivering all over. At the continuous shoving You receive, the thorns penetrate more and more into your most holy head. The Cross, with its heavy weight, digs into your shoulder, to the extent of forming a wound so deep that the bones are exposed. At every step, it seems that You are dying, and unable to move any further. But your love, which can do everything, gives You strength, and as You feel the Cross penetrate into your shoulder, You repair for the hidden sins; those which, not being repaired, increase the bitterness of your spasms. My Jesus, let me place my shoulder under the Cross to relieve You and repair with You for all hidden sins.

But your enemies, for fear that You may die under It, force the Cyrenean to help You carry the Cross. Unwilling and complaining, he helps You – not out of love, but by force. Then all the complaints of those who suffer, the lack of resignation, the rebellions, the anger and despising in suffering, echo in your Heart. But You remain even more pierced in seeing that souls consecrated to You, whom You call to be your help and companions in your suffering, escape You; and if You hug them to Yourself through suffering - ah, they wriggle free from your arms to look for pleasures, and so they leave You alone, suffering!

My Jesus, while I repair with You, I pray You to hold me in your arms, but so tightly that there may be no pain that You suffer in which I do not take part, so as to be transformed in them and make up for the abandonment of all creatures. My Jesus, overcome with weariness, all bent over, You can hardly walk; but I see that You stop and try to look. My Heart, what is it? What are You looking for? Ah, it is Veronica, who, fearless and courageous, with a cloth dries your Face all covered with blood, and You leave your Face impressed on it, as sign of gratitude. My generous Jesus, I too want to dry You, but not with a cloth; I want to expose all of myself to relieve You, I want to enter into your interior and give You, O Jesus, heartbeat for heartbeat, breath for breath, affection for affection, desire for desire. I intend to dive into your Most Holy Intelligence, and making all these heartbeats, breaths, affections and desires flow in the immensity of your Will, I intend to multiply them to infinity. I want, O my Jesus, to form waves of heartbeats, so that not one evil heartbeat may resound in your Heart, and so soothe all your interior bitternesses. I intend to form waves of affections and desires to cast away all evil affections and desires which might, even slightly, sadden your Heart. Still more, O my Jesus, I intend to form waves of breaths and thoughts, to cast away any breath or thought that could slightly displease You. I will be on guard, O Jesus, so that nothing else may afflict You, adding more bitterness to your interior pains. O my Jesus, please, let all of my interior swim in the immensity of yours; in this way I will be able to find enough love and will, so that no evil love may enter your interior, nor a will which may displease You.

O my Jesus, to be more certain, I pray You to seal my thoughts with Yours, my will with Yours, my desires with Yours, my affections and heartbeats with Yours; so that, being sealed, they may take no life but from You. I ask You, again, O my Jesus, to accept my poor body which I would want to tear to shreds for love of You, and reduce it to tiny little pieces, to place over each one of your wounds. On that wound, O Jesus, which gives You pain from so many blasphemies, I place a little piece of my body, wanting it to say to You constantly: "I bless You". On that wound that gives You so much pain from the many ingratitudes, I intend, O Jesus, to place a portion of my body, to prove my gratitude to You. On that wound, O Jesus, which makes You suffer so much from coldness and lack of love, I intend to place many little bits of my flesh, to say to You constantly: "I love You, I love You, I love You!" On that wound which gives You so much pain from the so many irreverences to your Most Holy Person, I intend to place a piece of myself, to tell You always: "I adore You, I adore You, I adore You!" O my Jesus, I want to diffuse myself in everything, and in those wounds embittered by the many misbeliefs, I desire that the shreds of my body tell You, always: "I believe - I believe in You, O my Jesus, my God, and in your Holy Church, and I intend to give my life to prove my Faith to You!" O my Jesus, I plunge myself into the immensity of your Will, and making It my own, I want to compensate for all, and enclose the souls of all in the power of your Most Holy Will. O Jesus, I still have my blood left, which I want to pour over your wounds as balm and soothing liniment, in order to relieve You and heal You completely. Again, I intend, O Jesus, to make my thoughts flow in the heart of every sinner, to reprimand him continuously, that he may not dare to offend You. And I pray to You with the voice of your Blood, so that all may surrender to my poor prayers. In this way I will be able to bring them into your Heart! Another grace, O my Jesus, I ask of You: that in everything I see, touch and hear, I may see, touch and hear always You; and that your Most Holy Image and your Most Holy Name, always be impressed in every particle of my poor being.

In the meantime, the enemies, disapproving of this act of Veronica, flog You, push You, and shove You on the way! A few more steps and You stop again. Even under the weight of so much suffering, your love does not stop, and on seeing the pious women weeping because of your pains, You forget Yourself and console them, saying: "Daughters, do not weep over my pains, but over your sins and over your children". What a sublime teaching, how sweet is your word! O Jesus, with You I repair for the lack of charity, and I ask You for the grace of making me forget myself, to remember nothing but You alone.

On hearing You speak, your enemies become furious, they pull You by the ropes, and push You with such rage as to make You fall. As You fall, You knock against the stones: the weight of the Cross crushes You, and You feel You are dying! Let me sustain You, and protect your most holy Face with my hands. I see You touch the ground and gasp in your Blood. But your enemies want to make You stand; they pull You by the ropes, they lift You by your hair, they kick You - but all in vain. You are dying, my Jesus! What pain - my heart breaks with grief! Almost dragging You, they take You up to Mount Calvary. As they drag You, I hear You repair for all the offenses of the souls consecrated to You, which weigh upon You so much that, as much as You try to stand, You cannot! And so, dragged and trampled upon, You reach Calvary, leaving behind You the red trace of your precious Blood.

**Jesus is stripped and crowned with thorns for the third time.**

But new sufferings await You here. They strip You again, tearing off both garment and crown of thorns. Ah, You groan in feeling the thorns being torn from inside your head. And as they pull your garment, they tear also the lacerated flesh attached to it. The wounds rip open, your Blood flows to the ground in torrents; the pain is such that, almost dead, You fall.

But nobody is moved to compassion for You, my Good! On the contrary, with bestial fury they put the crown of thorns on You again. They beat it on well, and the torture they cause You because of the lacerations and the tearing of your hair clotted in the coagulated blood, is such that only the Angels could tell what You suffer, while, horrified, they turn their celestial gaze away, and weep!

My stripped Jesus, allow me to hold You to my heart to warm You, as I see that You are shivering and an icy mortal sweat invades your Most Holy Humanity. How I would want to give You my life – my blood to take the place of yours, which You have lost to give me life!

In the meantime, barely looking at me with His languishing and dying eyes, Jesus seems to tell me: "My child, how much souls cost Me! This is the place where I wait for everyone in order to save them, where I want to repair for the sins of those who arrive at degrading themselves lower than beasts, and are so obstinate in offending Me as to reach the point of not being able to live without committing sins. Their minds remain blinded, and they sin wildly. This is why they crown Me with thorns for the third time. And by being stripped, I repair for those who wear luxurious and indecent clothing, for the sins against modesty, and for those who are so bound to riches, honors and pleasures, as to make of them a god for their hearts.

Ah, yes, each one of these offenses is a death that I feel; and if I do not die, it is because the Will of my Eternal Father has not yet decreed the moment of my death!"

My stripped Good, while I repair with You, I pray You to strip me of everything with your most holy hands, and not to allow that any bad affection may enter into my heart. Watch over it; surround it with your pains; fill it with your love. May my life be nothing but the repetition of Yours; strengthen my stripping with your blessing; bless me from your Heart, and give me the strength to be present at your sorrowful crucifixion, to remain crucified with You!

## REFLECTIONS AND PRACTICES
## by St. Hannibal di Francia

Jesus carries the Cross. The love of Jesus for the Cross, His anxious ardor to die on It for the salvation of souls, are immense! And we - do we love suffering like Jesus? Can we say that our heartbeats echo His divine heartbeats, and that we too ask for our cross?!

When we suffer, do we have the intention of becoming companions of Jesus in order to relieve Him from the weight of His Cross? How do we accompany Him? As He receives insults, are we always ready to give Him our little suffering as relief for His pains?

In working, in praying, and when we feel the hardship of our suffering under the weight of interior pains, do we let our pain fly to Jesus, which, like a veil, may dry up His sweat and cheer Him, as we make His hardship our own?

All: O my Jesus, call me always to be close to You, and remain always near me, so that I may comfort You always with my pains.

# The Nineteenth Hour

From 11 AM to 12 PM

## Jesus is Crucified

### First Part: The Crucifixion.

My Love, Jesus, You have already been stripped of your garments; your Most Holy Body is so lacerated that You look like a skinned lamb. I see You all shivering, and my heart breaks with pain in seeing You dripping Blood from all parts of your Most Holy Body! Your enemies, tired, but not satiated with tormenting You, in stripping You, tear the crown of thorns off of your head, to your unspeakable pain, and then again they drive it onto You, making You feel unheard-of spasms, as they add new more painful wounds to the first.

Ah, my Jesus, in this third crowning, You repair for the perfidy of man, and for his obstinacy in sin!

My Jesus, if love had not wanted You to suffer greater pains than these, You would certainly have died from the sharpness of the pain You suffered in this third crowning with thorns. But now I see that You can no longer bear that pain, and with your eyes covered with Blood, You look to see whether one, at least, would come close to You to sustain You in so much suffering and in such great confusion.

147

My sweet Good, my dear Life, here You are not alone as You were last night. There is your sorrowful Mama, who, heart-pierced by intense sorrow, suffers as many deaths for as many pains as You suffer! There also, are loving Magdalene and faithful John, who are mute with sorrow at the sight of your pains. Tell me my Love, who do You want, to sustain You in so much pain? Oh, please, let me come to You – I, who more than anyone else, feel the need to be near You in these moments. Dear Mama and the others give me their place, and here I am, O Jesus, I come to You. I hug You, and I pray You to lean your head upon my shoulder, to let me feel the piercings of your thorns, in order to repair for all the offenses of thought that creatures commit. My Love, please, hold me to Yourself; I want to kiss, one by one, the drops of Blood which flow down your most holy Face, and I pray You that each one of these drops may be light for every mind of creature, so that no one may offend You with evil thoughts.

Meanwhile, my Jesus, You look at the Cross that your enemies are preparing for Yout. You hear the blows of the hammer with which your executioners are forming the holes into which they will drive the nails that will hold You crucified. And your Heart beats, more and more strongly, jumping with divine inebriation, yearning to lay Yourself upon that bed of pain, to seal with your death the salvation of our souls. And I hear You say: "Please, O Cross, receive Me soon into your arms, I am impatient of waiting! Holy Cross, upon You I shall come to give completion to all. Hurry, O Cross, fulfill the burning desire that consumes Me, to give life to souls. Delay no more; I anxiously yearn to lay Myself upon You in order to open the Heavens to all my children.

Oh Cross, it is true that You are my martyrdom, but in a little while You will also be my victory and my most complete triumph; and through You I will give abundant inheritances, victories, triumphs and crowns to my children."

As Jesus is saying this, His enemies command Him to lay Himself upon It; and promptly He obeys, to repair for our disobedience.

My Love, before You lay Yourself on the Cross, allow me to hold You more tightly to my heart, and to kiss your loving and bleeding wounds. Hear me, O Jesus, I do not want to leave You; I want to come with You, to lay myself on the Cross and remain nailed to It with You. True love does not tolerate separation, and You will forgive the daring of my love. Concede that I be crucified with You. See, my tender Love, I am not the only one to ask this of You, but also your sorrowful Mama, inseparable Magdalene, faithful John: we all say to You that it would be more bearable to be nailed with You to Your Cross, than to see You crucified alone! Therefore, together with You I offer myself to the Eternal Father - identified with your Will, with your Heart, with your reparations and with all your pains.

Ah, it seems that my adored Jesus says to me: "My child, you have anticipated my love; this is my Will: that all those who love Me be crucified with Me. Ah, yes, come and lay yourself on the Cross with Me; I will give you life with my Life, I will hold you as the beloved of my Heart."

And now, my sweet Good, You lay Yourself on the Cross, looking with so much love and with so much sweetness at your executioners - who already hold nails and hammers in their hands ready to pierce You - as to make a sweet invitation to hasten the crucifixion. Indeed, with inhuman fury, they grab your right hand, hold the nail on your palm, and with blows of the hammer, make it come out the opposite side of the Cross. The pain You suffer is so great that You shiver, O my Jesus; the light of your beautiful eyes is eclipsed, and your most holy Face turns pale and looks like death.

Blessed right hand of my Jesus, I kiss you, I compassionate you, I adore you and I thank you for myself and for all. For as many blows as you receive, so many souls do I ask you to free, at this moment, from eternal damnation. As many drops of Blood as You shed, so many souls do I pray You to wash in this most precious Blood of Yours. O my Jesus, for the bitter pain You suffer, I ask You to open the Heavens to all, and to bless all creatures. May your blessing call all sinners to conversion, and all heretics and unbelievers to the light of the Faith.

Oh Jesus, my sweet Life, your torment has only begun, and here your executioners, having finished the nailing of your right hand, with unheard-of cruelty grab your left hand, and in order to make it reach the mark of the hole, with violence, pull it so much that the joints of your arms and shoulders are dislocated, and by the force of the pain, your legs too, are contracted and convulsed. Then, with

150

untiring fury, they nail it to the Cross as they did with the right one.


Left hand of my Jesus, I kiss you, I compassionate you, I adore you, I thank you, and, for the blows you receive and for the bitter pains you suffer while they drive the nail through, I ask you to concede, at this moment, liberation from Purgatory to the purging souls. Yes, O Jesus, for the Blood You shed from this hand, I pray You to extinguish the flames that burn these souls. May this Blood be refreshment and a healthy bath for all, such as to purge them from any stain and dispose them to the beatific vision. My Love and my All, for this sharp pain You suffer, I ask You to close hell to all souls, and to hold back the lightnings of Divine Justice irritated, alas, by our own sins! O Jesus, let Divine Justice be appeased, so that the divine chastisements may not pour down upon the earth, and treasures of Divine Mercy may be opened for the benefit of all. My Jesus, I place the world and all generations into your arms, and I pray You, O my sweet Love, with the voices of your own Blood, to deny no one your forgiveness, and by the merits of your most precious Blood, to concede to all the salvation of their souls! Do not exclude anyone, O Jesus!


My Love, Jesus, your enemies are not yet content. With diabolical fury, they grab your most holy feet, contracted by the great pain suffered in the tearing of your arms, and they pull them so much that your knees, your ribs and all the bones of your chest, are dislocated. My heart cannot sustain this, my dear Good; I see your beautiful eyes eclipsed and veiled with Blood, for the intensity of the pain. Your livid lips contort, your cheeks hollow, your teeth chatter, while your chest pounds rapidly. Ah, my Love, how willingly would I take your place to spare You so much pain! I want to place on every part of You a relief, a kiss, a comfort, a reparation for all.

My Jesus, they put your feet one on top of the other, and drive a nail without a point through them. Blessed feet of my Jesus, I kiss you, I adore you, I thank you; and for the most bitter pains you suffer, for the tearing and for the Blood you shed, I pray you to enclose all souls in your most sacred wounds.

O Jesus, do not disdain anyone! May your nails nail our powers, so that they may not move away from You; may they nail our hearts, so that they may always be fixed in You alone; may they nail all our feelings, so that they may have no taste which does not come from You. Oh my crucified Jesus, I see You all bleeding, as though swimming in a bath of Blood, which asks continuously for souls. By the power of this Blood, I ask You, O Jesus, that not one of them may escape You ever again!

Oh Jesus, I come close to your tortured Heart; I see that You cannot take any more, but Love cries out more loudly: "Pains, pains, more pains".

My Jesus, I hug You, I kiss You, I compassionate You, I adore You and I thank You for myself and for all. Jesus, I want to place my head upon your Heart, to feel what You feel in this painful Crucifixion. Ah, I hear every blow of the hammer echoing in It; everything is centered in It – from

It do your pains begin, and in It do they end. Ah, if it were not already decreed that a lance would rip your Heart, the flames of your love would open their way, and would make It explode! These flames call loving souls to find a happy dwelling in your Heart, and I, O Jesus, for the sake of your most precious Blood, ask You for sanctity for these souls. O please, do not allow them ever to go out from your Heart, and with your grace, multiply the vocations of victim souls, who may continue your life upon earth. You wanted to give a distinct place in your Heart to the loving souls; let them never lose this place. Oh Jesus, may the flames of your Heart burn me and consume me; may your Blood embellish me; may your love keep me always nailed to It through suffering and reparation.

O my Jesus, the executioners have now nailed your hands and feet to the Cross, and turning It over in order to bend the nails, they force your adorable Face to touch the ground, soaked with your own Blood; and You, with your divine lips, kiss it. With this kiss, O my sweet Love, You intend to kiss all souls and bind them to your love, placing a seal on their salvation. O Jesus, let me take your place, and while your executioners pound on the nails, let these blows wound me as well, and nail me completely to your love.

My Jesus, as the thorns are driven more and more into your head, I want to offer You, O my sweet Good, all my thoughts which, like loving kisses, may console You and soothe the bitterness of your thorns.

O Jesus, I see that your enemies are not yet satiated with insulting You and deriding You, and I want to comfort your divine gazes with my gazes of love.

Your tongue is almost attached to your palate because of the bitterness of the bile and the ardent thirst. In order to quench your thirst, O my Jesus, You would want all the hearts of creatures overflowing with love, but not having them, You burn more and more for them. My sweet Love, I intend to send You rivers of love, to soothe in some way the bitterness of the bile and your ardent thirst. O Jesus, I see that at every movement You make the wounds of your hands rip open more and more, and the pain becomes more intense and sharp. My dear Good, to relieve and soothe this pain I offer You the holy works of all creatures. O Jesus, how much You suffer in your most holy feet! It seems that all the movements of your Most Sacred Body pound in them, and nobody is near You to sustain You, and somehow soothe the bitterness of your sufferings! My most sweet Life, I would want to reunite the steps of creatures of all generations, past, present and future, and direct them all to You, to come to console You in your hard pains.

O my Jesus, alas, how tortured is your poor Heart! How to comfort so much pain? I will diffuse myself in You; I will place my heart in Yours, my ardent desires in Yours, so that any evil desire may be destroyed. I will diffuse my love in Yours, so that by means of your fire, the hearts of all creatures may be burned, and the profaned loves destroyed. Your Most Sacred Heart will be comforted, and from now on I promise You, O Jesus, always to remain nailed to this most loving Heart, with the nails of your desires, of your love and of your Will.

O my Jesus – Crucified You; crucified I in You. Do not allow me, even slightly, to unnail myself from You, but let me always be nailed to You to be able to love You and repair for all, and to soothe the pain which creatures give You with their sins.

## Second Part: Jesus Crucified. With Him we disarm Divine Justice.

My good Jesus, I see that your enemies lift the heavy wood of the Cross and let It drop into the hole they had prepared; and You, my sweet Love, remain suspended between Heaven and earth. In this solemn moment, You turn to the Father, and with weak and feeble voice, You say to Him: "Holy Father, here I am, loaded down with all the sins of the world. There is not one sin which does not pour upon Me; therefore, no longer unload the scourges of your Divine Justice upon man, but upon Me, your Son. O Father, allow Me to bind all souls to this Cross, and to plead forgiveness for them with the voices of my Blood and of my wounds. O Father, do You not see how I have reduced Myself? By this Cross, by virtue of these pains, concede true conversion, peace, forgiveness and sanctity to all. Arrest your fury against poor humanity, against my children. They are blind, and know not what they are doing. Look well at Me, how I have reduced Myself because of them; if You are not moved to compassion for them, may You at least be softened by this Face of mine, dirtied with spit, covered with Blood, bruised and swollen by the so many slaps and blows received. Have pity, my

Father! I was the most beautiful of all, and now I am all disfigured, to the point that I no longer recognize Myself. I have become the abject of all; and so, at any cost, I want to save the poor creature!"

My Jesus, how is it possible that You love us so much? Your love crushes my poor heart. Oh, I would want to go into the midst of all creatures to show this Face of Yours, so disfigured because of them, to move them to compassion for their own souls and for your love; and with the light which emanates from your Face, and with the enrapturing power of your love, make them understand who You are, and who they are, who dare to offend You, so that they may prostrate themselves before You, to adore You and glorify You.

My Jesus, adorable Crucified, the creature continues to irritate Divine Justice, and with her tongue, she makes resound the echo of horrible blasphemies, voices of curses and maledictions, and evil discourses. Ah, all these voices deafen the earth, and penetrating even into the Heavens, while deafening the divine hearing, they curse and ask for revenge and justice against her! Oh, how Divine Justice feels pressed to hurl Its scourges! Oh, how the many horrendous blasphemies ignite Its fury against the creature! But You, O my Jesus, loving us with highest love, face these deadly voices with your omnipotent and creative voice, and cry out for mercy, graces and love for the creature. In order to appease the indignation of the Father, all love, You say to Him: "My Father, look at Me once again, do not listen to the voices of the creatures, but to mine; I am the One who satisfies for all. Therefore I pray You to look at the creature, and to look at her in Me; if You look at her outside of Me, what will happen to her? She is weak, ignorant, capable only of doing evil, and full

156

of miseries. Have pity – pity on the poor creature. I answer for her with my tongue embittered by bile, parched by thirst, dried and burned by love."

My embittered Jesus, my voice in Yours wants to face all these offenses, all the blasphemies, in order to change all human voices into voices of blessings and praises.

My Crucified Jesus, at so much love and pain of yours, the creature does not yet surrender; on the contrary, she despises You and adds sins to sins, committing enormous sacrileges, murders, suicides, duels, frauds, deceits, cruelties and betrayals. Ah, all these evil works weigh on the arms of your Celestial Father; so much so, that unable to sustain their weight, He is about to lower them and pour fury and destruction upon the earth. And You, O my Jesus, to snatch the creature from the divine fury, fearing to see her destroyed - You stretch out your arms to the Father, You disarm Him, and prevent Divine Justice from taking Its course. And to move Him to compassion for miserable Humanity and to soften Him, You say to Him with the most persuasive voice: "My Father, look at these hands, ripped open, and the nails that pierce them, which nail them together with all these evil works. Ah, in these hands I feel all the spasms that these evil works give to Me. Are You not content, O my Father, with my pains? Am I perhaps not capable of satisfying You? Yes, these dislocated arms of mine will always be chains to hold the poor creatures tightly, so that they may not escape from Me, except for those who wanted to struggle free by sheer force. These arms of mine will be loving chains that will bind You, my Father, to prevent You from destroying the poor creature. Even more, I will draw You closer and closer to her, that You may pour your graces and mercies upon her!"

My Jesus, your love is a sweet enchantment for me, and pushes me to do what You do. So, together with You, at the cost of any pain, I want to prevent Divine Justice from taking Its course against poor Humanity. With the Blood that pours out of your hands I want to extinguish the fire of sin that ignites It, and to calm Its fury. Allow me to place in your arms, the sufferings and the torments of all men, and the many hearts, grieving and oppressed. Allow me to go among all creatures and press them all into your arms, so that all of them may return to your Heart. By the power of your creative hands, allow me to stop the current of so many evil works, and to hold everyone back from doing evil.

My lovable crucified Jesus, the creature is not yet content in offending You. She wants to drink, to the bottom, all the filth of sin, and she runs almost wildly along the path of evil. She falls from sin to sin, disobeys all of your Laws, and denying You, rebels against You, and almost out of spite, she wants to go to hell. Oh, how indignant becomes the Supreme Majesty! And You, O my Jesus, triumphing of everything, even over the obstinacy of creatures, in order to appease the Divine Father, show Him all of your Most Holy Humanity, lacerated, dislocated, tortured in a horrible way. You show your most holy feet, pierced, twisted by the atrocity of the spasms, and I hear your voice, more moving than ever, as though in act of breathing its last, wanting to conquer the creature by force of love and pain, and to triumph over the Paternal Heart: "My Father, look at Me, from head to foot; there is not one part of Me which is left whole. I do not know

158

where else to let them open more wounds and to procure more sufferings. If You do not placate Yourself at this sight of love and suffering, who will ever be able to appease You? O creatures, if you do not surrender to so much love, what hope remains for you to convert? These wounds and Blood of Mine will be voices that constantly call from Heaven to earth, graces of repentance, forgiveness and compassion for you!"

My Jesus, Crucified Lover, I see that You can take no more. The terrible tension that You suffer on the Cross, the continual creaking of your bones that dislocate more and more at every tiny movement, your flesh that rips more and more, the ardent thirst that consumes You, the interior pains that suffocate You with bitterness, pain and love - and, in the face of so many martyrdoms, the human ingratitude that insults You and penetrates, like a mighty wave, into your pierced Heart, oppress You so much that your Most Holy Humanity, unable to bear the weight of so many martyrdoms, is about to end, and raving with love and suffering, cries out for help and pity! Crucified Jesus, is it possible that You, who rule everything and give life to all, ask for help? Ah, how I wish to penetrate into each drop of your most precious Blood, and to pour my own in order to soothe each one of your wounds, to lessen and render less painful the pricks of each thorn, and into every interior pain of your Heart to relieve the intensity of your bitternesses. I wish I could give You life for life. If it were possible, I would want to unnail You from the Cross and put myself in your place; but I see that I am nothing and can do nothing - I am too insignificant. Therefore, give me Yourself; I will take life in You, and in

You, I will give You Yourself. In this way You will satisfy my yearnings. Tortured Jesus, I see that your Most Holy Humanity is ending, not because of You, but to fulfill our Redemption in everything. You need divine aid, and so You throw Yourself into the Paternal arms and ask for help and assistance. Oh, how moved is the Divine Father in looking at the horrible torture of your Most Holy Humanity, the terrible crafting that sin has made upon your most holy members! And to satisfy your yearnings of love, He holds You to His Paternal Heart, and gives You the necessary helps to accomplish our Redemption; and as He holds You tightly, You feel again in your Heart, more intensely, the blows of the nails, the lashes of the scourging, the tearing of the wounds, the pricking of the thorns. Oh, how the Father is struck! How indignant He becomes in seeing that all these pains are given to You, up into your inmost Heart, even by souls consecrated to You! And in His sorrow, He says to You: "Is it possible, my Son, that not even the part chosen by You is wholly with You? On the contrary, it seems that these souls ask for refuge and a hiding place in your Heart in order to embitter You and give You a more painful death. And even more, all these pains they give to You, are hidden and covered by hypocrisy. Ah, Son, I can no longer contain my indignation at the ingratitude of these souls, who grieve Me more than all the other creatures together!"

But You, O my Jesus, triumphing of everything, defend also these souls, and with the immense love of your Heart, form a shield to the waves of bitternesses and piercings that these souls give You. And to appease the Father, You say to Him: "My Father, look at this Heart of Mine. May all these pains satisfy You; and the more bitter they are, the more powerful may they be over your Heart of Father, to plead graces, light and forgiveness for them. My Father, do not reject them; they will be my defenders who will continue my life upon earth."


My Life, Crucified Jesus, I see You still agonizing on the Cross, because your love is not yet satisfied in order to give completion to all. I too, yes, agonize together with You. And all of you, Angels and Saints – come to Mount Calvary, to admire the excesses, and the follies of the love of a God! Let us kiss His bleeding wounds; let us adore them; let us sustain those lacerated limbs; let us thank Jesus for the accomplished Redemption. Let us turn our gaze to the pierced Mother, who feels pains and deaths in Her Immaculate Heart, for as many pains as She sees in Her Son God. Her own clothes are soaked with His Blood; Mount Calvary is all covered with It. So, all together, let us take this Blood, let us ask the sorrowful Mother to unite Herself to us; let us divide ourselves throughout the whole world, and let us go to the help of all. Let us help those who are in danger, that they may not perish; those who have fallen, that they may stand up again; those who are about to fall, that they may not fall. Let us give this Blood to the many poor blind, that the light of truth may shine in them. In a special way, let us go into the midst of the poor soldiers, to be their vigilant sentries, and if they are about to be struck by the lead of the enemy, let us receive them into our arms, to comfort them. And if they are abandoned by all, if they are desperate with their sad destiny, let us give them this Blood that they may be resigned, and the atrocity of the pain lessened. And if we see that there are souls who are about to fall into hell, let us give them this Divine Blood, which contains the price of Redemption - let us snatch them from Satan! And while I hold Jesus tightly to my heart in order to defend Him and shelter Him from everything, I will hold everyone to this Heart, so that all may obtain effective grace of conversion, strength and salvation.

Meanwhile, O Jesus, I see that your Blood flows in torrents from your hands and from your feet. The Angels, weeping, surrounding You like a crown, admire the portents of your immense love. I see your sweet Mama, pierced by pain, at the foot of the Cross; your dear Magdalene, beloved John – all taken by ecstasy of awe, love and pain! O Jesus, I unite myself to You and I cling to your Cross; I take all the drops of your Blood and I pour them into my heart.

When I see your Justice irritated against sinners, I will show You this Blood in order to appease You. When I want the conversion of souls obstinate in sin, I will show You this Blood, and by virtue of It You will not reject my prayer, because I hold its pledge in my hands. And now, my Crucified Good, in the name of all generations, past, present and future, together with your Mama and with all the Angels, I prostrate myself before You and say: "We adore You, O Christ, and we bless You, because by your Holy Cross You have redeemed the world."

## REFLECTIONS AND PRACTICES
## by St. Hannibal di Francia

Crucified Jesus obeys His executioners. He accepts with love all the insults and pains which they give Him. Jesus found in the Cross His bed of rest for the great love which He felt for our poor soul. And we - do we rest in Him in all our pains? Can we say that we prepare a bed for Jesus in our heart with our patience and with our love?

While Jesus is being crucified, there is not one interior or external part of Him which does not feel a special suffering. Do we remain completely crucified to Him, at least with our main senses? When we find our enjoyment in a futile conversation or in some other similar amusement, then it is Jesus that remains nailed to the cross. But if we sacrifice that same taste for love of Him, then we remove the nails from Jesus, and pierce ourselves.

Do we always keep our mind, our heart and all of our being as nailed with the nails of His Most Holy Will? While being crucified, Jesus looks at His executioners with love. Do we look with love at those who offend us, for love of Him?

All: My crucified Jesus, may your nails be driven into my heart, so that there may be no heartbeat, affection or desire which does not feel their pricking; and may the blood which this heart of mine will shed, be the balm that soothes all of your wounds.

## Twentieth Hour

From 12 to 1 PM

**First Hour of Agony on the Cross.**

The first word of Jesus

My Crucified Good, I see You on the Cross, as on the Throne of your triumph, in the act of conquering everything and all hearts, and of drawing them so closely to You, that all may feel your superhuman power. Horrified at such great crime, nature prostrates itself before You, and waits in silence for a word from You, to pay You honor and let your dominion be recognized. The sun, crying, withdraws its light, unable to sustain your sight, too sorrowful. Hell is terrified and waits in silence. Everything is silence. Your pierced Mama, your faithful ones, are all mute; and petrified at the sight of your torn and dislocated Humanity - alas, too painful, they are silently waiting for a word from You. Your very Humanity is silent, lying in a sea of pains, among the harrowing spasms of agony; so much so that they fear You are going to die at each breath!

What more? Even the perfidious Jews and the ruthless executioners who, up to a little while ago, were offending You, mocking You, calling You impostor, criminal; even the thieves who were cursing You – everyone is silent, mute. Remorse invades them, and if they try to launch an insult against You, it dies on their lips.

But as I penetrate into your interior, I see that love overflows; it suffocates You and You cannot contain it. And forced by your love that torments You more than the pains themselves, with strong and moving voice, You speak as the God You are; You raise your dying eyes to Heaven, and exclaim: "Father, forgive them, for they know not what they are doing!" And, again, You close Yourself in silence, immersed in unheard-of pains.

Crucified Jesus, how can so much love be possible? Ah, after so many pains and insults, your first word is of forgiveness; and You excuse us before the Father for so many sins! Ah, You make this word descend into each heart after sin, and You are the first to offer forgiveness. But how many reject it and do not accept it; your love is then taken by follies, because You anxiously desire to give your forgiveness and the kiss of peace to all!

At this word, hell trembles and recognizes You as God; nature and everyone remain astonished; they recognize your Divinity, your inextinguishable love, and silently wait to see where it reaches. And not only your voice, but also your Blood and your wounds, cry out to every heart after sin: "Come into my arms, for I forgive you, and the seal of forgiveness is the price of my Blood." O my lovable Jesus, repeat this word again to all the sinners which are in the world. Beseech mercy for all; apply the infinite merits of your most precious Blood for all. O good Jesus, continue to placate Divine Justice for all, and concede your grace to those who, finding themselves in the act of having to forgive, do not feel the strength to do it.

My Jesus, adored Crucified, in these three hours of most bitter agony, You want to give fulfillment to everything; and while, silent, You remain on this Cross, I see that in your interior You want to satisfy the Father in everything. You thank Him for all, You satisfy Him for all, You beseech forgiveness for all, and for all You impetrate the grace that they may never again offend You. In order to impetrate this from the Father You go through all of your life, from the first instant of your conception, up to your last breath. My Jesus, endless Love, let me go through all your life together with You, with the inconsolable Mama, with Saint John, and with the pious women.

Let us go through the Life and the pains of Jesus.

My sweet Jesus, I thank You for the many thorns that pierced your adorable head, for the drops of Blood shed by It, for the blows You received on It, and for the hair they tore from You. I thank You for all the good You have done and impetrated for all, for the enlightenments and the good inspirations You have given us, and for all the times You have forgiven all of our sins of thought, of pride, of conceit and of self-esteem. I ask your forgiveness in the name of all, O my Jesus, for all the times we have crowned You with thorns; for all the drops of Blood we made You shed from your most sacred head; for all the times we have not corresponded to your inspirations. For the sake of all these pains suffered by You, I ask You, O Jesus, to impetrate for us the grace to never again commit sins of thought. I also intend to offer You everything You suffered in your most holy head, in order to give You all the glory that the creatures would have given You, had they made good use of their intelligence.

O my Jesus, I adore your most holy eyes, and I thank You for all the tears and the Blood they have shed, for the cruel pricks of the thorns, for the insults, the derisions and the contempts You bore during all of your Passion. I ask your forgiveness for all those who use their sight to offend You and insult You, asking You, for the sake of the pains suffered in your most sacred eyes, to give us the grace that no one may ever again offend You with evil gazes. I also intend to offer You all that You Yourself suffered in your most holy eyes, to give You all the glory that the creatures would have given You if their gazes were fixed only on Heaven, on the Divinity and on You, O my Jesus.

I adore your most holy ears; I thank You for all that You suffered while those wicked people on Calvary deafened them with shouts and mockeries. I ask your forgiveness in the name of all for all the evil discourses which are listened to, and I pray that the ears of all men may be opened to the eternal truths, to the voices of Grace, and that no one may offend You, ever again, with the sense of hearing. I also intend to offer You all that You suffered in your most holy hearing, to give You all the glory that the creatures would have given You, had they made holy use of this organ.

O my Jesus, I adore and I kiss your most holy Face, and I thank You for all that You suffered from the spit, the slaps and the mockeries received, and for all the times You allowed Yourself to be trampled by your enemies. I ask your forgiveness in the name of all, for all the times we have dared to offend You, asking You, for the sake of these slaps and this spit, to let your Divinity be recognized, praised and glorified by all. Even more, O my Jesus, I myself intend to go throughout the whole world, from the east to the west, from the south to the north, to unite all the voices of the creatures and change them into as many acts of praise, of love and of adoration. Also, O my Jesus, I intend to bring You all the hearts of the creatures, so that You may cast light, truth, love and compassion for your Divine Person into all. And as You forgive all, I ask You not to allow anyone to offend You, ever again; if possible, even at the cost of my blood. Finally, I intend to offer You everything You suffered in your most holy Face, to give You all the glory that the creatures would have given You, if no one had dared to offend You.

I adore your most holy mouth, and I thank You for your first wails, for the milk You suckled, for all the words You said, for the ardent kisses You gave to your Most Holy Mother, for the food You took, for the bitterness of the gall and of the ardent thirst You suffered on the Cross, and for the prayers You raised to the Father. I ask your forgiveness for all the gossip and the evil and mundane discourses made by creatures, and for all the blasphemies they utter. I intend to offer your holy discourses in reparation for their evil discourses; the mortification of your taste to repair for their gluttonies, and for all the offenses they have given You with an evil use of their tongue. I intend to offer You everything You suffered in your most holy mouth, to give You all the glory that the creatures would have given You, if none of them had dared to offend You with the sense of taste and with the abuse of their tongue.

O Jesus, I thank You for everything, and in the name of all, I raise to You a hymn of eternal and infinite thanksgiving. O my Jesus, I intend to offer You everything You have suffered in your Most Holy Person, to give You all the glory that the creatures would have given You, had they conformed their lives to Yours.

I thank You, O Jesus, for everything You have suffered in your most holy shoulders, for all the blows You have received, for all the wounds You have allowed them to open on your Most Sacred Body, and for all the drops of Blood You have shed. I ask your forgiveness in the name of all, for all the times in which, for love of comforts, they have offended You with illicit and evil pleasures. I offer You your painful scourging to repair for all the sins committed with all the senses, for love for one's own tastes, for sensible pleasures, for one's own self and all natural satisfactions. I also intend to offer You all that You have suffered in your shoulders, to give You all the glory that the creatures would have given You, if they had tried to please You alone in everything, and to find shelter under the shadow of your divine protection.

My Jesus, I kiss your left foot; I thank You for all the steps You took during your mortal life, and for all the times You tired your poor limbs, going in search of souls to lead to your Heart. Therefore, O my Jesus, I offer You all of my actions, steps and movements, with the intention of giving You reparation for everything and for everyone. I ask your forgiveness for those who do not operate with righteous intention; I unite my actions to yours in order to divinize them, and I offer them united to all the works

You did with your Most Holy Humanity, to give You all the glory that the creatures would have given You, had they operated in a saintly way and with upright purposes.

O my Jesus, I kiss your right foot, and I thank You for all You have suffered and do suffer for me, especially in this hour, in which You are hanging on the Cross. I thank You for the excruciating crafting that the nails are making in your wounds, which rip open more and more at the weight of your Most Sacred Body. I ask your forgiveness for all the rebellions and disobediences committed by creatures, offering You the pains of your most holy feet in reparation for these offenses, to give You all the glory that the creatures would have given You, had they been submitted to You in everything.

O my Jesus, I kiss your most holy left hand; I thank You for all that You have suffered for me, for all the times You have placated the Divine Justice, satisfying for everything! I kiss your right hand, and I thank You for all the good You have done, and You do, for all. In a special way, I thank You for the works of Creation, of Redemption and of Sanctification. I ask your forgiveness in the name of all, for all the times we have been ungrateful at your benefits, for our many works done without upright intention. In reparation for all these offenses, I intend to give You all the perfection and sanctity of your works, to give You all the glory that the creatures would have given You, had they corresponded to all of these benefits.

O my Jesus, I kiss your Most Sacred Heart, and I thank You for all You have suffered, desired and yearned for, for love of all and for each one in particular. I ask your forgiveness for the many evil desires, and for the affections and tendencies which are not good – forgiveness, O Jesus, for many who place your love after the love of creatures. And to give You all the glory that these have denied You, I offer You everything that your most adorable Heart has done and continues to do.

## REFLECTIONS AND PRACTICES
## by St. Hannibal di Francia

Jesus, raised on the Cross, remains suspended without touching the earth. And we - do we try to live detached from the world, from creatures, and from everything that tastes of earth? Everything must concur to form the cross on which we must lay ourselves, and remain suspended like Jesus, far away from all that is earth, so that creatures may not be attached to us.

Suffering Jesus has no other bed than the Cross, no other relief than wounds and insults. Does our love for Jesus reach the extent of finding rest in suffering? Let us enclose everything we do - prayers, sufferings and other things - in those wounds. Let us dip everything in the Blood of Jesus, and we will find comfort nowhere but in His pains. Therefore, the wounds of Jesus will be ours; His Blood will work continuously in us in order to cleanse us and embellish us; in this way we will draw all graces for ourselves and for the salvation of souls. With the deposit of the Blood of Jesus in our heart, if we commit any error, we will pray Jesus not to keep us dirty in His presence, but to wash us with His Blood, and keep us always together with Him. If we feel weak, we will pray Jesus to give a sip of His Blood to our souls, so as to give us strength. Sweet Jesus prays for His executioners; even more, He excuses them. Do we make the prayer of Jesus our own in order to continuously excuse sinners before the Father, and to plead mercy for them, even for those who may have offended us?

While we pray, work or walk, let us also not forget the poor souls who are about to give their last breath. Let us bring the prayers and kisses of Jesus to their aid and comfort, so that His most precious Blood may purify them, and let them take flight toward Heaven.

All: My Jesus, from your wounds and from your Blood, I want to draw strength in order to repeat your own life in Me. In this way, I will be able to plead for all, the good which You Yourself did.

# Twenty-first Hour

From 1 to 2 PM

## Second Hour of Agony on the Cross.

Second, third and fourth word of Jesus

Second word on the Cross.

My pierced Love, while I pray with You, the enrapturing power of your love and of your pains keeps my gaze fixed on You. But my heart breaks in seeing You suffer so much. You agonize with love and with pain, and the flames that burn your Heart rise so high as to be in the act of reducing You to ashes. Your constrained love is stronger than death itself; and wanting to pour it out, looking at the thief on your right, You steal him from Hell. With your grace You touch his heart, and that thief is completely changed; he recognizes You; he professes You God, and all contrite, says: "Lord, remember me when You are in your Kingdom." And You do not hesitate to answer: "Today you will be with Me in Paradise", making of him the first triumph of your love.

But I see that, in your love, You are not stealing the heart of that thief alone, but also that of many who are dying! Ah, You place your Blood, your love, your merits at their disposal, and You use all divine devices and stratagems in order to touch their hearts and steal them all for Yourself. But, also here, your love is hindered! How many rejections, how much lack of trust, how much desperation! And the pain is such that, again, it reduces You to silence!

O my Jesus, I intend to repair for those who despair of the Divine Mercy at the point of death. My sweet Love, inspire trust and unlimited confidence in You for all, especially for those who find themselves in the grips of agony; and by virtue of your word, concede to them light, strength and help, to be able to die in a saintly way, and fly from this earth up to Heaven. O Jesus, enclose all souls – all of them, in your Most Holy Body, in your Blood, in your wounds. And by the merits of this most precious Blood of Yours, do not allow even one soul to be lost! Together with your voice, may your Blood cry out for all, again: "Today you will be with Me in Paradise."

Third word on the Cross.

My Jesus, tortured Crucified, your pains increase more and more. Ah, on this Cross You are the true King of Sorrows. In the midst of so many pains, not one soul escapes You; even more, You give your own life to each one of them. But your love sees itself hindered, despised, neglected by creatures, and unable to pour itself out, it becomes more intense – it gives You unspeakable tortures. In these tortures, it keeps investigating for what else it can give to man; and to conquer him, it makes You say: "Look, O soul, how much I have loved you. If you do not want to have pity on yourself, at least have pity on my love!" In the meantime, seeing that You have nothing else to give him, because You have given him everything, You turn your languid gaze to your Mama. She too is more than dying because of your pains; and the love that tortures Her is so great as to render Her crucified like You. Mother and Son - You understand each other, and You sigh with satisfaction and feel comforted in seeing that You can give your Mama to the creature; and considering the whole Mankind in John, with a voice so sweet as to move all hearts, You say: "Woman, behold your son"; and to John: "Behold your Mother." Your voice descends into Her maternal Heart, and united to the voices of your Blood, it keeps saying: "My Mother, I entrust all of my children to You; feel for them all the love that You feel for Me. May all your maternal cares and tendernesses be for my children. You will save them all for Me." Your Mama accepts. In the meantime, the pains are so intense that, again, they reduce You to silence.

O my Jesus, I intend to repair for the offenses given to the Most Holy Virgin, for the blasphemies and the ingratitudes of many who do not want to recognize the benefits You have granted by giving Her to us as Mother.

How can we thank You for such a great benefit? O Jesus, we turn to your own source and we offer You your Blood, your wounds, the infinite love of your Heart! O Most Holy Virgin, how moved You are, in hearing the voice of good Jesus, leaving You to us as Mother!

We thank You, O blessed Virgin, and in order to thank You as You deserve, we offer You the very thanksgivings of your Jesus. O sweet Mama, be our Mother, take care of us, and do not allow us to offend You even slightly. Keep us always clasped to Jesus; with your hands bind us – all of us, to Him, that we may not escape Him, ever again. With your own intentions, I intend to repair for all, for the offenses given to your Jesus and to You, my sweet Mama!

O my Jesus, while You are immersed in so many pains, You plead even more the salvation of souls. But I will not remain indifferent; like a dove, I want to take flight onto your wounds, kissing them, soothing them, and diving into your Blood, to be able to say, with You: "Souls, souls!" I want to sustain your pierced and sorrowful head, to repair and ask for mercy, love and forgiveness for all.

Reign in my mind, O Jesus, and heal it by virtue of the thorns that pierce your head; and do not allow any disturbance to enter into me. Majestic forehead of my Jesus, I kiss you; draw all of my thoughts to contemplate You and to comprehend You. Most sweet eyes of my Good, though covered with Blood, look at me – look at my misery, look at my weakness, look at my poor heart, and let it experience the admirable effects of your divine gaze. Ears of my Jesus, though deafened by the insults and the blasphemies of the wicked, and yet intent on listening to us – O please, listen to my prayers and do not disdain my reparations. Yes, O Jesus, listen to the cry of my heart; only when You have filled it with your love, then will it be calmed. Most beautiful Face of my Jesus, show Yourself – let me see You, that I may detach my poor heart from everyone and from everything. May your beauty enamor me continuously, and keep me always enraptured within You. Most sweet mouth of my Jesus, speak to me; may your voice always resound in me, and may the power of your word destroy all that is not Will of God - all that is not love.

O Jesus, I extend my arms around your neck in order to embrace You; and You, extend Yours to embrace me. Please, O my Good, let this embrace of love be so tight, that no human strength may be able to unbind us. And while we are embraced like this, I will place my face upon your Heart, and then, with trust, I will kiss your lips, and You will give me your kiss of love. So You will make me breathe your most sweet breath, your love, your Will, your pains, and all of your Divine Life. Most holy shoulders of my Jesus, always strong and constant in suffering for love of me, give me the strength, the constancy and the heroism to suffer for love of Him.

O Jesus, please, do not allow that I be inconstant in love; on the contrary, let me share in your immutability! Enflamed breast of my Jesus, give me your flames; You can no longer contain them, and my heart anxiously searches for them through that Blood and those pains. It is the flames of your love, O Jesus, that torment You the most. O my Good, let me take part in them; does a soul so cold and poor in your love not move You to compassion? Most holy hands of my Jesus, you who have created Heaven and earth, are now reduced to being unable to move! O my Jesus, continue your creation – the creation of love. Create new life – Divine Life, in all my being; pronounce your words over my poor heart, and transform it completely into Yours. Most holy feet of my Jesus, never leave me alone; allow me always to run with you, and to take not one step away from you. Jesus, with my love and with my reparations, I intend to relieve You from the pains You suffer in your most holy feet.

O my Jesus Crucified, I adore your most precious Blood; I kiss your wounds one by one, intending to profuse in them all my love, my adorations, my most heartfelt reparations. May your Blood be for all souls, light in darkness, comfort in sufferings, strength in weakness, forgiveness in guilt, help in temptations, defense in dangers, support in death, and wings to carry them all from this earth up to Heaven.

O Jesus, I come to You, and in your Heart I form my nest and my home. O my sweet Love, I will call everyone to You from within your Heart; and if anyone wants to draw near to offend You, I will expose my breast, and I will not permit him to wound You; even more, I will enclose him in your Heart; I will speak about your love, and I will make the offenses turn into love.

O Jesus, do not allow me ever to leave your Heart; feed me with your flames, and give me life with your Life, that I may love You as You Yourself yearn to be loved.

Fourth word on the Cross.

Suffering Jesus, while I remain abandoned, clinging to your Heart and counting your pains, I see that a convulsive trembling invades your Most Holy Humanity. Your limbs are shaking, as if one wanted to detach from the other; and amid contortions, because of the atrocious spasms, You cry out loudly: "My God, my God, why have You abandoned Me?" At this cry, everyone trembles; the darkness becomes thicker; your Mama, petrified, turns pale and faints!

My Life! My All! My Jesus, what do I see? Ah, You are about to die; your very pains, so faithful to You, are about to leave You. And at the same time, after so much suffering, with immense sorrow You see that not all souls are incorporated in You. Rather, You see that many will be lost, and You feel the painful separation of them, as they detach themselves from your limbs. And You, having to satisfy Divine Justice also for them, feel the death of each one of them, and the very pains they will suffer in hell. And You cry out loudly, to all hearts: "Do not abandon Me. If you want more pains, I am ready – but do not separate yourselves from my Humanity. This is the sorrow of sorrows – it is the death of deaths; everything else would be nothing, if I did not have to suffer your separation from Me! O please, have pity on my Blood, on my wounds, on my death! This cry will be continuous to your hearts. O please, do not abandon Me!"

My Love, how I grieve together with You! You are panting; your most holy head drops on your breast – life is abandoning You.

My Love, I feel I am dying; I too want to cry out with You: "Souls, souls!" I will not detach myself from this Cross, from these wounds, so that I may ask for souls. And if You want, I will descend into the hearts of creatures, I will surround them with your pains, so that they may not escape me. And if it were possible, I would like to place myself at the gate of hell, to make the souls who are destined to go there, draw back, and to conduct them to your Heart. But You agonize and remain silent, and I cry over your nearing death. O my Jesus, I compassionate You, I press your Heart tightly to mine, I kiss It, and I look at It with all the tenderness I am capable of; and to give You a greater relief, I make the divine tenderness my own, and with it I intend to compassionate You, change my heart into rivers of sweetness and pour it into Yours, to soothe the bitterness You feel because of the loss of souls. This cry of yours, O my Jesus is, alas, painful; more than the abandonment of the Father, it is the loss of the souls who move far away from You that makes this painful lament escape from your Heart! O my Jesus, increase grace in everyone, that no one may be lost; and may my reparation be for the good of those souls who should be lost, that they may not be lost.

I also pray You, O my Jesus, for the sake of this extreme abandonment, to give help to so many loving souls, whom You seem to deprive of Yourself, leaving them in the dark, to have them as companions in your abandonment. O Jesus, may their pains be like prayers that call souls near to You, and relieve You in your pain.

## REFLECTIONS AND PRACTICES
## by St. Hannibal di Francia

Jesus forgives the good thief, and with so much love as to bring him immediately to Paradise with Himself. And we - do we pray always for the souls of the so many dying who need a prayer, so that hell may be closed to them, and the gates of Heaven be opened?

The pains of Jesus on the Cross increase but, forgetful of Himself, He always prays for us. He leaves nothing for Himself, giving everything to us, even His Most Holy Mother, offering Her as the dearest gift from His Heart. And we - do we give everything to Jesus?

In all that we do - prayers, actions and other things - do we always have the intention of absorbing new love within ourselves, so as to give everything back to Him? We must absorb it in order to give it, so that everything we do may carry the seal of the works of Jesus.

When the Lord gives us fervor, light and love, do we use them for the good of others? Do we try to enclose souls in this light and in this fervor, so as to move the Heart of Jesus to convert them; or do we selfishly keep His graces for ourselves alone?

O my Jesus, may every little spark of love that I feel in my heart become a fire which may consume all the hearts of creatures, and enclose them in your Heart.

What use do we make of the great gift of His Mama, whom He gave to us? Do we make the love of Jesus, the tendernesses of Jesus and all that Jesus did our own, so as to make His Mama content? Can we say that our divine Mother finds in us the contentment that She found in Jesus? Are we always close to Her, as faithful children; do we obey Her and imitate Her virtues? Do we try every way in order not to escape from Her maternal gaze, so that She may keep us always clinging to Jesus? In everything we do, do we always call the gazes of the celestial Mother to guide us, so as to be able to act in a saintly way, as true children of Hers, under Her compassionate gaze? In order to give Her the same contentment as Her Son gave to Her, let us ask from Jesus all the love that He had for His Most Holy Mother, the glory that He continuously gave to Her, His tenderness and all His finesses of love. Let us make all this our own, and let us say to the Celestial Mama: 'We have Jesus in ourselves; and in order to make You content, so that You may find in us all that You found in Jesus, we give everything to You. Moreover, beautiful Mama, we also want to give to Jesus all the contentments that He found in You. Therefore, we want to enter into your Heart and take all your love, all your contentments, all your tendernesses and maternal cares, and give them all to Jesus. Our Mama, may your maternal hands be the sweet chains which keep us bound to You and to Jesus.'

Jesus does not spare Himself in anything. Loving us with highest love, He would want to save us all and, if it were possible, snatch all souls from hell, even at the cost of suffering all of their pains. In spite of this, He sees that, through continual strain, the souls want to free themselves from His arms and, unable to contain His pain, He cries out: "My God, my God, why have You abandoned Me?" And we - can we say that our love for souls is similar to that of Jesus? Are our prayers, our pains and all of our most tiny acts united to the acts and to the prayers of Jesus in order to snatch souls from hell? How do we compassionate Jesus in His immense sorrow? If our life could be consumed in a continuous holocaust, it would not be enough to compassionate this sorrow. Every little act, suffering and thought that we do united to Jesus can be used to grab souls, so that they may not fall into hell. United with Jesus, we will have His own power in our hands. But if we do not do our acts united with Jesus, they will not serve to prevent even one soul from going to hell.

My Love and my All, hold me tightly to your Heart, so that I may feel immediately how much the sinner saddens You in detaching himself from You, and therefore be able to do my part immediately. O my Jesus, may your love bind my heart, so that, burned by your fire, I may feel the love that You Yourself had for souls. When I suffer sorrows, pains and bitternesses, then pour out your Justice upon me, O Jesus, and take the satisfaction You want. But may the sinner be saved, O Jesus; may my pains be the bond which binds You and the sinner; and may my soul receive the consolation of seeing your Justice satisfied.

## Twenty-second Hour

From 2 to 3 PM

**Third Hour of Agony on the Cross.**

Fifth, sixth and seventh word of Jesus. The death of Jesus

Fifth word on the Cross.

O my dying Crucified, clinging to the Cross, I feel the fire that burns all of your Most Holy Person. Your Heart beats so strongly that, pushing out your ribs, it torments You in such a harrowing and horrible way, that all your Most Holy Humanity undergoes a transformation which renders You unrecognizable. The love that enflames your Heart withers You and burns You completely; and You, unable to contain it, feel the intense torment, not only of the corporal thirst, but of the shedding of all your Blood – and even more, of the ardent thirst for the salvation of our souls. You would want to drink us like water, in order to place us all in safety within Yourself; therefore, gathering your weakened strengths, You cry out: "I thirst". Ah, You repeat this voice to every heart: "I thirst for your will, for your affections, for your desires, for your love. A water fresher and sweeter than your soul you could not give Me. O please, do not let Me burn. My thirst is ardent, such that I not only feel my tongue and my throat burn, to the point that I can no longer utter a word, but I also feel my Heart and bowels wither. Have pity on my thirst – have pity!"

And as though delirious from the great thirst, You abandon Yourself to the Will of the Father.

Ah, my heart can no longer live in seeing the evil of your enemies who, instead of water, give You gall and vinegar; and You do not refuse them! Ah, I understand – it is the gall of the many sins, it is the vinegar of our untamed passions that they want to give You, which, instead of refreshing You, burn You even more. O my Jesus, here is my heart, my thoughts, my affections – here is all of my being, to quench your thirst and give a relief to your mouth, dried and embittered.

Everything I have, everything I am – everything is for You, O my Jesus. Should my pains be necessary in order to save even one soul alone – here I am, I am ready to suffer everything. I offer myself wholly to You - do with me whatever You best please.

I intend to repair for the sorrow You suffer for all the souls who are lost, and for the pain You receive from those who, while You allow sadnesses and abandonments, instead of offering them to You as relief for the burning thirst that devours You, abandon themselves to themselves, and make You suffer even more.

Sixth word on the Cross.

My dying Good, the endless sea of your pains, the fire that consumes You, and more than anything, the Supreme Will of the Father which wants You to die, no longer allow us to hope that You may continue to live. And I - how shall I live without You? Your strengths are now leaving You, your eyes become veiled, your face is transformed and covered with mortal paleness; your mouth is half- open, your breath is labored and interrupted, to the point that there is no more hope that You may revive. A chill and a cold sweat which wets your forehead, take over the fire that burns You. Your muscles and nerves contract more and more because of the bitterness of the pains and the piercings of the nails; the wounds rip open more; and I tremble – I feel I am dying. I look at You, O my Good, and I see the last tears descend from your eyes, bearers of your nearing death; while You, with difficulty, let another word be heard: "All is consummated."

O my Jesus, You have now exhausted Yourself completely; You have nothing left – love has reached its end. And I – have I consumed myself completely in your love? What thanksgiving shall I not render to You? What shall my gratitude not be for You? O my Jesus, I intend to repair for all – repair for the lack of correspondence to your love, and console You for the offenses You receive from creatures, while You are consuming Yourself with love on the Cross.

Seventh word on the Cross.

My dying Crucified, Jesus, You are now about to give the last breaths of your mortal life; your Most Holy Humanity is already stiffened; your Heart seems to beat no longer.

With Magdalene I cling to your feet and, if it were possible, I would like to give my life to revive Yours.

Meanwhile, O Jesus, I see that You open your dying eyes again, and You look around from the Cross, as though wanting to give the last good-bye to all. You look at your dying Mama, who no longer has motion or voice, so many are the pains She feels; and You say: "Good-bye Mama, I am leaving, but I will keep You in my Heart. You, take care of my children and yours." You look at crying Magdalene, faithful John and your very enemies, and with your gazes You say to them: "I forgive you; I give you the kiss of peace." Nothing escapes your gaze; You take leave of everyone and forgive everyone. Then, You gather all your strengths, and with a loud and thundering voice, You cry out: "Father, into your hands I commend my spirit". And bowing your head, You breathe your last.

My Jesus, at this cry all nature is shaken and cries over your death – the death of its Creator! The earth trembles strongly; and with its trembling, it seems to be crying and wanting to shake up souls to recognize You as true God. The veil of the Temple is torn, the dead are risen; the sun, which until now had cried over your pains, has withdrawn its light with horror. At this cry, your enemies fall on their knees, and beating their breasts, they say: "Truly He is the Son of God." And your Mother, petrified and dying, suffers pains harder than death.

My dead Jesus, with this cry You also place all of us into the hands of the Father, because You do not reject us. Therefore You cry out loudly, not only with your voice, but with all your pains and with the voices of your Blood: "Father, into your hands I commend my spirit and all souls." My Jesus, I too abandon myself in You; give me the grace to die completely in your love - in your Will, and I pray that You never permit me, either in life or in death, to go out of your Most Holy Will. Meanwhile I intend to repair for all those who do not abandon themselves perfectly to your Most Holy Will, therefore losing or maiming the precious gift of your Redemption. What is not the sorrow of your Heart, O my Jesus, in seeing so many creatures escaping from your arms and abandoning themselves to themselves? Have pity on all, O my Jesus - have pity on me.

I kiss your head crowned with thorns, and I ask your forgiveness for my many thoughts of pride, of ambition and of self-esteem. And I promise You that every time a thought arises in me which is not completely for You, O Jesus, and that I find myself in occasions of offending You, immediately I will cry out: "Jesus and Mary, I commend my soul to You."

O Jesus, I kiss your beautiful eyes, still wet with tears and covered with dried Blood, and I ask your forgiveness for all the times I have offended You with evil and immodest gazes. I promise You that every time my eyes are led to look at things of the earth, immediately I will cry out: "Jesus and Mary, I commend my soul to You."

O my Jesus, I kiss your most sacred ears, deafened by insults and horrible blasphemies up to the very last moments, and I ask your forgiveness for all the times I have listened to, or made others listen to discourses which move us away from You, and for all the evil discourses made by creatures. I promise You that every time I find myself in the occasion of hearing unseemly discourses, immediately I will cry out: "Jesus and Mary, I commend my soul to You."

O my Jesus, I kiss your most holy Face, pale, bruised and bleeding, and I ask your forgiveness for the many scorns, offenses and insults You receive from us, most miserable creatures, with our sins. I promise You that every time I have the temptation of not giving You all the glory, the love and the adoration which is due to You, immediately I will cry out: "Jesus and Mary, I commend my soul to You."

O my Jesus, I kiss your most sacred mouth, dry and embittered. I ask your forgiveness for all the times I have offended You with my evil discourses; for all the times I have contributed to embittering You and increasing your thirst. I promise You that every time the thought comes to me of making discourses which might offend You, immediately I will cry out: "Jesus and Mary, I commend my soul to You."

O my Jesus, I kiss your most holy neck, and I can still see the marks of the chains and ropes which have oppressed You. I ask your forgiveness for the many bonds and the many attachments of the creatures, which have increased the ropes and the chains around your most holy neck. And I promise You that every time I feel disturbed by attachments, desires and affections which are not for You, immediately I will cry out: "Jesus and Mary, I commend my soul to You."

My Jesus, I kiss your most holy shoulders, and I ask your forgiveness for the many illicit satisfactions; forgiveness for the many sins committed with the five senses of our body. I promise You that every time the thought comes to me of taking some pleasures or satisfactions which are not for your glory, immediately I will cry out: "Jesus and Mary, I commend my soul to You."

My Jesus, I kiss your most holy breast, and I ask your forgiveness for all the coldness, indifference, luke-warmness and horrendous ingratitude You receive from the creatures; and I promise You that every time I feel my love for You become cooler, immediately I will cry out: "Jesus and Mary, I commend my soul to You."

My Jesus, I kiss your most sacred hands. I ask your forgiveness for all the evil and indifferent works; for many acts rendered malicious by love of self and self-esteem. I promise You that every time the thought comes to me of not operating only for love of You, immediately I will cry out: "Jesus and Mary, I commend my soul to You."

O my Jesus, I kiss your most holy feet, and I ask your forgiveness for the many steps, the many paths covered without righteous intention; for many who move away from You to go in search of the pleasures of the earth. I promise You that every time the thought comes to me of moving away from You, immediately I will cry out: "Jesus and Mary, I commend my soul to You."

O Jesus, I kiss your Most Sacred Heart, and I intend to enclose in It, with my soul, all the souls redeemed by You, so that all may be saved – no one excluded.

O Jesus, lock me in your Heart, and close the doors, that I may see nothing but You. I promise You that every time the thought comes to me of wanting to go out of this Heart, immediately I will cry out: "Jesus and Mary, to You I give my heart and my soul."

## REFLECTIONS AND PRACTICES
## by St. Hannibal di Francia

Jesus burns with thirst. Do we burn with thirst for Jesus? Do our thoughts and affections have always the purpose of quenching His ardent thirst?

Unable to bear the thirst that consumes Him, thirsty Jesus adds: "All is consummated!" So, Jesus consumed Himself completely for us. And we - do we strive, in each thing, to be a continuous consummation of love for Jesus? Each act, word and thought led Jesus toward His consummation. Do all of our acts, words and thoughts move us to be consumed for love of Jesus?

O Jesus, sweet Life of mine, may your consumed breath always blow in my poor heart, that I may receive the mark of your consummation.

On the Cross Jesus fulfills the Will of the Father in everything, and He breathes His last with a perfect act of abandonment in His Most Holy Will. Do we fulfill the Will of God in everything? Do we abandon ourselves perfectly in His Volition without looking at whether it is advantageous for us or not - just being content to find ourselves abandoned in His most holy arms? Is our dying to ourselves continuous for love of Jesus? Can we say that, although we live, we do not live; that we are dead to everything in order to live not from our own life, but only from the life of Jesus? Does everything we do, think, desire and love call the living of Jesus within us, so as to make our word, our step, our desire and our thought die completely in Jesus?

O my Jesus, may my death be a continuous death for love of You, and may each death I suffer be a life which I intend to give to all souls.

# Twenty-third Hour

From 3 to 4 PM

**Jesus, dead, is pierced by the thrust of a lance.**

The deposition from the Cross

My dead Jesus, all nature has sent out a cry of sorrow at your last breath, and has cried over your sorrowful death, recognizing You as its Creator. The Angels, thousands upon thousands, hover around the Cross, and cry over your death. They adore You as our true God, and accompany You to Limbo, where You go to beatify many souls who have been ardently longing for You for centuries upon centuries. My dead Jesus, I cannot pull myself away from your Cross, nor can I be satiated of kissing and kissing again your most holy wounds, which eloquently speak to me of how much You have loved me. In seeing the horrendous tearings, the depth of your wounds, to the point of uncovering your bones – ah, I feel I am dying! I would like to cry so much over these wounds as to wash them with my tears. I would like to love You so much as to heal You completely with my love, and restore the natural beauty of your unrecognizable Humanity. I would like to open my veins to fill your empty veins with my blood and call You back to life.

O my Jesus, what can love not do? Love is life, and with my love I want to give You life; and if mine is not enough, give me your love. With your love, I will be able to do anything – yes, I will be able to give life to your Most Holy

194

Humanity. O my Jesus, even after your death You want to show me that You love me, prove your love for me, and give me a refuge, a shelter, in your Sacred Heart. Therefore, pushed by a supreme force, to be assured of your death, a soldier rips your Heart open with a lance, opening a profound wound. And You, my Love, shed the last drops of Blood and water contained in your enflamed Heart.

Ah, how many things does this wound, opened by love, tell me! And if your mouth is mute, your Heart speaks to me, and I hear It say: "My child, after I gave everything, I wanted this lance to open a shelter for all souls inside this Heart of Mine. Opened, It will cry out to all, continuously: Come into Me if you want to be saved. In this Heart you will find sanctity and you will make yourselves saints; you will find relief in afflictions, strength in weakness, peace in doubts, company in abandonments. O souls who love Me, if you really want to love Me, come to dwell in this Heart forever. Here you will find true love in order to love Me, and ardent flames for you to be burned and consumed completely in love. Everything is centered in this Heart: here are the Sacraments, here my Church, here the life of my Church and the life of all souls. In It I also feel the profanations made against my Church, the plots of the enemies, the arrows they send, and my oppressed children – there is no offense which my Heart does not feel. Therefore, my child, may your life be in this Heart – defend Me, repair Me, bring Me everyone into It."

My Love, if a lance has wounded your Heart for me, I pray that You too, with your own hands, wound my heart, my affections, my desires – all of myself. Let there be nothing in me which is not wounded by your love. I unite everything to the harrowing pains of our dear Mama, who, for the pain of seeing your Heart being ripped open, falls into a swoon of sorrow and love; and like a dove, She flies in It to take the first place – to be the first Repairer, the Queen of your very Heart, the Mediatrix between You and the creatures. I too, with my Mama, want to fly into your Heart, to hear how She repairs, and to repeat Her reparations for all the offenses You receive. O my Jesus, in this wounded Heart of Yours, I will find my life again; therefore, anything I may be about to do, I will always draw from It. I will no longer give life to my thoughts; but if these want life, I will take Yours. My will will no longer have life; but if it wants life, I will take your Most Holy Will. My love will no longer have life; if it wants life, I will take your Love. O my Jesus, all of your Life is mine – this is your Will, this is my will.

Jesus is deposed from the Cross.

My dead Jesus, I see that your disciples hasten to depose You from the Cross. Joseph and Nicodemus, who have remained hidden until now, with courage and without fearing anything, now want to give You an honorable burial. So they take hammers and pincers, to perform the sacred and sad unnailing from the Cross, while your pierced Mama stretches out Her maternal arms to receive You on Her lap.

My Jesus, while they unnail You, I too want to help your disciples to sustain your Most Holy Body; and with the nails they remove from You, nail me completely to

Yourself. With your Holy Mother, I want to adore You and kiss You, and then enclose myself in your Heart, never to leave again.

## REFLECTIONS AND PRACTICES
## by St. Hannibal di Francia

After His death, Jesus wanted to be wounded by a lance for love of us. And we - do we let ourselves be wounded in everything by the love of Jesus; or do we rather let ourselves be wounded by the love of creatures, by pleasures, and by attachment to ourselves? Also coldness, obscurity and mortifications, both interior and external, are wounds which the Lord makes to the soul. If we do not take them from the hands of God, we wound ourselves, and our wounds increase passions, weaknesses, self- esteem - in a word, every evil. On the other hand, if we take them as wounds made by Jesus, He will place His love, His virtues and His likeness in these wounds, which will make us deserve His kisses, His caresses and all the stratagems of a divine love. These wounds will be continuous voices which will call Him and force Him to dwell with us continuously.

O my Jesus, may your lance be my guard which defends me from any wound of creatures. Jesus allows Himself to be deposed from the Cross into the arms of His Mama. And we - do we deposit all of our fears, our doubts and our anxieties in the arms of our Mama? Jesus rested on the lap of His divine Mother. Do we let Jesus rest by casting away our fears and our agitations?

All: My Mama, with your maternal hands remove from my heart all that may prevent Jesus from resting in me.

# Twenty-fourth Hour

From 4 to 5 PM

**The Burial of Jesus.**

Most Holy Desolate Mary

My sorrowful Mama, I see that You dispose Yourself to the final sacrifice of having to give burial to your lifeless Son Jesus. Most resigned to the Will of God, You accompany Him, and You place Him in the sepulcher with your own hands. But as You compose those limbs and are about to give Him the last good-bye and the last kiss, You feel your Heart being torn from your breast because of the pain. Love nails You to those limbs, and by force of love and sorrow, your life is about to fade together with your lifeless Son. Poor Mama, how shall You go on without Jesus? He is your Life your All. Yet, it is the Will of the Eternal One that wants it so. You will have to fight with two insurmountable powers: Love and Divine Will. Love nails You, in such a way that You cannot separate from Him; the Divine Will imposes Itself and wants the sacrifice. Poor Mama, how shall You go on? How much compassion I feel for You! O please, Angels of Heaven, come to raise Her from the stiffened limbs of Jesus, otherwise She will die!

But, oh portent, while She seemed to be extinguished together with Jesus, I hear Her voice, trembling and interrupted by sobs, say: "Beloved Son, O Son, this was the only relief which was left to Me, and which halved my pains: your Most Holy Humanity - pouring Myself out on these wounds, adoring them, kissing them. Now this too is taken away from Me, because the Divine Will wants it so; and I resign Myself. But know, Son, that I want it and I can not. At the mere thought of doing it, my strengths leave Me and life runs away from Me. Oh please, O Son, so that I may have life and strength to be able to depart, allow Me to remain all buried in You, and to take for Myself your Life, your pains, your reparations, and all that You are. Ah, only an exchange of Life between You and Me can give Me the strength to make the sacrifice of departing from You!"

So determined, my afflicted Mama, I see that You go through those limbs again, and You place your head in the head of Jesus. Kissing it, You enclose in it your thoughts, and You take for Yourself His thorns, His afflicted and offended thoughts, and everything He suffered in His most holy head. Oh, how You would want to animate the Intelligence of Jesus with your own, to be able to give life for life! You now begin to feel revived, by having taken the thoughts and the thorns of Jesus into your mind.

Sorrowful Mama, I see You kiss the lifeless eyes of Jesus, and I feel pierced in seeing that Jesus no longer looks at You. How many times His gazes filled You with Paradise, and made You rise again from death to life; and now, not seeing Yourself gazed upon, You feel You are dying! Therefore You place your eyes in those of Jesus, and You take for Yourself His eyes, His tears, and His bitternesses in seeing the offenses of creatures, and the many insults and scorns.

But I see, my pierced Mama, that You kiss His most holy ears, and You call Him over and over again, saying: "My Son, how can it be that You no longer listen to Me – You, who would hear my slightest motion? And now I cry, I call You, and You do not hear Me? Ah, love is the most cruel tyrant! You were more than my own life for Me, and now I will have to survive so much pain? Therefore, O Son, I leave my hearing in Yours, and I take for Myself what You have suffered in your most holy hearing, and the echo of the offenses that resounded in it. Only this can give Me life – your pains, your sorrows!" And as You say this, the pain and the grip on your Heart is so great, that You lose your voice and remain motionless. My poor Mama, my poor Mama, how much compassion I feel for You! How many cruel deaths You suffer!

But the Divine Will imposes Itself and gives You motion; and You look at His most holy Face, You kiss it, and exclaim: "Adored Son, how disfigured You are! Ah, if love did not tell Me that You are my Son, my Life, my All, I would no longer recognize You, so unrecognizable You are! Your beauty was transformed into deformity; your cheeks into bruises, and the light, the grace of your Face – which was such that seeing You and remaining beatified was the same thing - has turned into paleness of death, O beloved Son. Son, how You are reduced! What an awful crafting sin has made upon your most holy limbs! Ah, how much would your inseparable Mama want to give You back your original beauty! I want to fuse my face in Yours, and take for Myself your Face, and the slaps, the spit, the scorns, and everything You have suffered in your most holy Face. Ah, Son, if You want Me alive, give Me your pains; otherwise I will die!"

And your pain is so great that it suffocates You, it breaks your speech, and You remain as though lifeless on the Face of Jesus. Poor Mama, how much compassion I feel for You! My Angels, come to comfort my Mama; Her sorrow is immense – it inundates Her, it suffocates Her, and leaves Her no more life or strength. But the Divine Will, breaking through these waves, gives life back to Her.

You are now at the mouth of Jesus, and in kissing it, You feel your lips embittered by the gall which so much embittered His mouth; and sobbing, You continue: "Son, say one last word to your Mama. How can it be that I will no longer be able to listen to your voice? All of the words You have spoken to Me in life, like many arrows, wound my Heart with sorrow and with love. And now, seeing You mute, they put themselves in motion once again within my lacerated Heart; they give Me many deaths, and would want to snatch, by force, one last word from You. But not receiving it, they torment Me, and they say to Me: 'So, You will no longer hear Him; You will no longer hear His sweet accent, the melody of His creative word!' He created as many Paradises in Me as words that He spoke. Ah, my Paradise is finished, and I will have nothing but bitternesses! Ah, Son, I want to give You my tongue in order to animate Yours. Give Me that which You suffered in your most holy mouth – the bitterness of the gall, your ardent thirst, your reparations and prayers; and so hearing your voice through them, my sorrow will be more bearable, and your Mama will be able to live through your pains."

Tormented Mama, I see You hasten, because those who surround You want to close the sepulcher. Almost flying, You take the hands of Jesus between yours, You kiss them, You press them to your Heart; and placing your hands in His, You take for Yourself the pains and the piercings of those most holy hands. Then You fly over the feet of Jesus, looking at the cruel torture which the nails have made in them; and as You place your feet in them, You take for Yourself those wounds, and You offer Yourself to run toward sinners in the place of Jesus, in order to snatch them from hell.

Anguishing Mama, I see You give the last good-bye to the pierced Heart of Jesus. Here You pause. It is the last assault to your maternal Heart; You feel It being torn from your breast because of the vehemence of love and pain and, by Itself, It runs to place Itself in the Most Holy Heart of Jesus. And You, in seeing Yourself without a heart, hasten to take His Most Holy Heart into yours - His love rejected by many creatures, His many ardent desires not fulfilled because of their ingratitudes, and the pains and piercings of that Most Holy Heart, which will keep You crucified for the rest of your life. In looking at the wide wound, You kiss it, You lap up the Blood; and feeling the Life of Jesus in Yourself, You have the strength to fulfill the bitter separation. Then You embrace Him, and You allow the sepulchral stone to close on Him.

My Sorrowful Mama, crying, I pray You not to allow, for now, that Jesus be taken away from our gaze. Wait for me to first enclose myself in Jesus, in order to take His Life within me. If You, who are the Spotless, the All Holy, the Full of Grace, cannot live without Jesus, much less can I do it, who am weakness, misery, and full of sins. How can I live without Jesus? Sorrowful Mama, do not leave me alone, take me with You; but first place all of myself in Jesus. Empty me of everything, in order to place all of Jesus within me, just as You placed Him within Yourself. Begin with me the maternal office which Jesus has given You on the Cross; let my extreme poverty break through your maternal Heart, and with your own hands, enclose me completely in Jesus.

Enclose the thoughts of Jesus in my mind, so that no other thought may enter into me. Enclose the eyes of Jesus within mine, that He may never escape from my gaze; and His hearing in mine, that I may always listen to Him and do His Most Holy Will in everything. Place His Face within mine, so that, by looking at Him so disfigured for love of me, I may love Him, compassionate Him, and repair; His tongue in mine, that I may speak, pray and teach with the tongue of Jesus; His hands in mine, so that each movement I make and each work I perform may have life from the works and actions of Jesus. Place His feet in mine, so that each one of my steps may be a life of salvation, of strength and of zeal for the other creatures.

And now, my afflicted Mama, allow me to kiss His Heart and to lap up His most precious Blood; You Yourself, enclose His Heart in mine, that I may live of His love, of

His desires, of His pains. Lastly, take the stiffened right hand of Jesus, that He may give me the last blessing.

The stone closes the sepulcher. Tortured, You kiss it, and crying, You give Him the last good-bye and depart. But your pain is so great, that You remain almost petrified as your blood runs cold. My pierced Mama, together with You, I say good-bye to Jesus; and crying, I want to compassionate You and accompany You in your bitter desolation. I want to place myself at your side, to give You a word of comfort, a gaze of compassion at each sigh, strain and sorrow of yours. I will gather your tears, and I will sustain You in my arms, if I see You faint.

But I see that You are forced to return to Jerusalem along the path from which You came. After only a few steps, You are already before the Cross on which Jesus suffered so much, and died. You run to embrace It, and in seeing It colored with Blood, the pains that Jesus suffered on It are renewed in your Heart, one by one. Unable to contain the pain, You exclaim: "O Cross, how could You be so cruel with my Son? Ah, You have spared Him nothing! What wrong had He done to You? You have not permitted Me, His sorrowful Mama, to give Him even a sip of water, while He was asking for it; and to His parched mouth You gave gall and vinegar! I felt my pierced Heart melt, and I wanted to offer It to His lips to quench His thirst, but I had the sorrow of seeing Myself rejected. O Cross, cruel, yes, but holy, because divinized and sanctified by contact with my Son! Turn that cruelty which You used with Him into compassion for miserable mortals; and for the sake of the pains He suffered on You, impetrate grace and strength for the souls who suffer, so that not one of them may be lost because of tribulations and crosses. Souls cost Me too much – they cost Me the life of a Son God; and as Co-Redemptrix and Mother, I bind them to You, O Cross." And after kissing It over and over again, You leave.

Poor Mama, how much compassion I feel for You! At each step and encounter, new pains arise, which increase in their immensity and become more bitter; they inundate You, they drown You; and You feel You are dying at each instant. You are now at the point at which You met Him this morning – exhausted, under the enormous weight of the Cross, dripping Blood, and with a bundle of thorns on His head, which, bumping against the Cross, penetrated deeper and deeper, giving Him pains of death at each blow. In crossing your gaze, the gaze of Jesus looked for pity; but the soldiers, pushed Him and made Him fall to deny You this comfort, making Him shed new Blood. You see the ground soaked with It; You throw Yourself to the ground, and as You kiss that Blood, I hear You say: "My Angels, come to place yourselves as guardians of this Blood, so that not one drop of It may be trodden upon and profaned."

Sorrowful Mama, allow me to give You my hand to lift You and raise You, because I see You faint on the Blood of Jesus. As You walk, You find new sorrows. Everywhere You see traces of Blood, and You remember the pains of Jesus; so You hasten your step and enclose Yourself in the Cenacle. I too enclose myself in the Cenacle - but my Cenacle is the Most Holy Heart of Jesus; from there I want to come to You, to keep You company in this hour of bitter desolation. My heart cannot bear leaving You alone in so much sorrow.

But I feel pierced in seeing that, as You move your head, You feel the thorns You have taken from Jesus penetrate into it – the pricks of all our sins of thought which, penetrating even into your eyes, make You cry tears of blood. Since You have the sight of Jesus in your eyes, all the offenses of creatures pass before your sight. How embittered You remain! How You comprehend all that Jesus has suffered, having His own pains within You! But one pain does not wait for another. As You prick up your ears, You feel deafened by the echo of the voices of creatures and from the variety of these offenses which reach your Heart and pierce It; and You say: "Son, how much You have suffered!"

Desolate Mama, how much compassion I feel for You! Allow me to dry your face, wet with tears and with blood. But I feel like drawing back on seeing it now covered with bruises, unrecognizable and pale with mortal paleness. I understand – these are the mistreatments against Jesus which You have taken upon Yourself, and which make You suffer so much that, as You move your lips in prayer or as your enflamed breast sighs, You feel your breath embittered and your lips burned by the thirst of Jesus. Poor Mama, how much compassion I feel for You! Your sorrows increase ever more, and as I take your hands in mine, I see them pierced by nails. It is in your hands that You feel the pain and see the murders, the betrayals, the sacrileges and all the evil works, repeating the blows, widening the wounds and embittering them more and more. How much compassion I feel for You! You are the true crucified Mother, so much so, that not even your feet remain without nails; even more, You feel them not only being pierced, but torn by many iniquitous steps, and by

206

the souls who go to hell. And You run after them, that they may not fall into the infernal flames.

But this is not all, pierced Mama. All of your pains, uniting together, echo in your Heart and pierce It - not with seven swords, but with thousands and thousands of swords. More so, since You have the Divine Heart of Jesus within You, which contains all hearts, and whose heartbeat encloses the heartbeats of all; and in beating, It says: "Souls! Love!". And from the heartbeat "Souls!", You feel all sins flow in your heartbeat, and death being inflicted on You; while in the heartbeat "Love!", You feel life being given to You. Therefore, You are in a continuous act of death and of life.

Crucified Mama, as I look at You, I compassionate your sorrows – they are unspeakable. I would like to transform my being into tongue and voice in order to compassionate You; but before so much pain, my compassion is nothing. Therefore I call the Angels, the very Sacrosanct Trinity, and I pray Them to place their harmonies, their contentments and their beauty around You, to soothe and compassionate your intense sorrows; to sustain You in their arms, and to requite all of your pains with love.

And now, desolate Mama, I thank You in the name of all for everything You have suffered; and I ask You, for the sake of your bitter desolation, to come to my assistance at the moment of my death. When I find myself alone and abandoned by all, in the midst of a thousand anxieties and fears – come then, to return to me the company which I have given You many times in life. Come to my assistance;

place Yourself beside me, and put the enemy to flight. Wash my soul with your tears, cover me with the Blood of Jesus, clothe me with His merits, embellish me and heal me with your sorrows and with all the pains and works of Jesus; and by virtue of them, let all my sins disappear, giving me total forgiveness. And as I breathe my last, receive me into your arms, place me under your mantle, hide me from the gaze of the enemy, take me straight to Heaven, and place me in the arms of Jesus. Let us make this agreement, my dear Mama!

And now, I pray You to return the company I have given You to all those who are agonizing. Be the Mama of all; these are extreme moments, and great aids are needed. Therefore, do not deny your maternal office to anyone.

One last word: as I leave You, I pray You to enclose me in the Most Sacred Heart of Jesus; and You, my sorrowful Mama, be my sentry, so that Jesus may not put me out of It; and I, even if I wanted, may not be able to leave. So I kiss your maternal hand; and You, bless me.

## REFLECTIONS AND PRACTICES
### by St. Hannibal di Francia

Jesus is buried. A stone seals Him and prevents His Mama from looking at Her Son any longer. And we - do we hide from the gazes of creatures; are we indifferent if everyone forgets us? In holy things, do we remain indifferent, with that holy indifference which makes us never disobey? In the total abandonment of Jesus, do we conquer everything with a holy indifference which leads us

208

continuously to Him? And do we form with our constancy a sweet chain, so as to draw Him toward us? Is our gaze buried in the gaze of Jesus, so that we look at nothing but that which Jesus wants? Is our voice buried in the voice of Jesus, so that if we want to speak, we do not speak but with the tongue of Jesus? Are our steps buried in His, so that as we walk, we may leave the mark of the steps of Jesus, not of our own? And is our heart buried in His, in order to love and desire as His Heart loves and desires?

My Mama, when Jesus hides from me for the good of my soul, give me the grace that You had in the privation of Jesus, so that I may give Him all the glory that You gave Him, when He was placed in the Sepulcher.

O Jesus, I want to pray to You with your voice. And just as your voice penetrated into the Heavens and resounded in the voices of all, in the same way, honoring your voice, may my voice penetrate even into Heaven, to give You the love and the glory of your own word.

My Jesus, my heart palpitates, but I am not content if You do not let me palpitate with your Heart; with your heartbeat, I will love as You love. I will give You the love of all creatures, and one will be the cry: 'Love, Love...!' O my Jesus, give honor to Yourself, and in everything I do, place the seal of your own power, of your love and of your glory.

## Selected chapters about the Passion of Our Lord Jesus Christ

from the Writings of Luisa Piccarreta

The Divine Passion of Jesus

Introductory Note: The Divine Passion of Our Lord, as Jesus teaches us in these Writings, is the Passion which the Divinity Itself inflicted on the Humanity of Jesus. This Passion, which is beyond human comprehension, is revealed by Jesus to Luisa and opens a new and immense horizon for the understanding, contemplation and meditation of the unheard-of sufferings of the Incarnate Word for the Redemption of mankind, which go far beyond His corporal Passion on the last day of His life, and His moral Passion due the ingratitude and rejection of man. The Divine Passion of Jesus began at the moment of His Incarnation and lasted His whole life. Mary Most Holy, who lived from that very Divine Will which, out of love for man, inflicted these pains on the Incarnated Word, was fully aware of it and took part in it.

Jesus to Luisa Piccarreta – Corato / Bari Italy

November 9, 1906 Volume 7

Effects of meditating continuously on the Passion.

Finding myself in my usual state, I was thinking about the Passion of Our Lord; and while I was doing this, He came and told me: "My daughter, one who meditates continuously on my Passion and feels sorrow for it and compassion for Me, pleases Me so much that I feel as though comforted for all that I suffered in the course of my Passion; and by always meditating on it, the soul arrives at preparing a continuous food. In this food there are many different spices and flavors, which form different effects. So, if in the course of my Passion they gave Me ropes and chains to tie Me, the soul releases Me and gives Me freedom. They despised Me, spat on Me, and dishonored Me; she appreciates Me, cleans Me of that spittle, and honors Me. They stripped Me and scourged Me; she heals Me and clothes Me. They crowned Me with thorns, mocking Me as king, embittered my mouth with bile, and - 12 - crucified Me; while the soul, meditating on all my pains, crowns Me with glory and honors Me as her king, fills my mouth with sweetness, giving Me the most delicious food, which is the memory of my own works; and unnailing Me from the Cross, she makes Me rise again in her heart. And every time she does so, I give her a new life of grace as recompense. She is my food, and I become her continuous food. So, the thing that pleases Me the most is meditating continuously on my Passion."

March 24, 1913 Volume 11

The continuous thought of His Passion.

I add that I was thinking to myself about the sweet Mama, and Jesus told me: "My daughter, the thought of my Passion never escaped my dear Mama, and by dint of repeating it, she filled all of Herself with Me, completely. The same happens to the soul: by dint of repeating what I suffered, she arrives at filling herself with Me."

April 10, 1913 Volume 11

The recompense for those who do the Hours of the Passion.

This morning my always lovable Jesus came, and hugging me to His Heart, told me: "My daughter, one who always thinks about my Passion forms a fount within her heart, and the more she thinks about It, the larger this fount becomes. And just as the waters that spring up are waters common to everyone, in the same way, this fount of my Passion which is formed in her heart serves for the good of the soul, for my glory, and for the good of all creatures." And I: 'Tell me, my Good, what will You give as recompense to those who will do the Hours of the Passion the way You taught them to me?' And He: "My daughter, I will look at these Hours, not as yours, but as done by Me. I will give you my same merits, as if I were in the act of suffering my Passion; and the same effects, according to the dispositions of the souls. This, while they are on earth - and I could not give them a greater reward. Then, in

Heaven, I will place these souls in front of Me, darting through them with darts of love and of contentments for as many times as they did the Hours of my Passion; and they will dart through Me. What a sweet enchantment this will be for all the Blessed!"

September 6, 1913 Volume 11

The Hours of the Passion are the very prayers of Jesus.

I was thinking about the Hours of the Passion, which have now been written, and how they are without any indulgence. So, those who do them gain nothing, while there are many prayers enriched with many indulgences. While I was thinking of this, my always lovable Jesus, all kindness, told me: "My daughter, through the prayers with indulgences one gains something, but the Hours of my Passion, which are my very prayers, my reparations, and all love, have come out of the very depth of my Heart. Have you perhaps forgotten how many times I have united Myself with you to do them together, and I have changed chastisements into graces over the whole earth? So, my satisfaction is such and so great, that instead of the indulgence, I give the soul a handful of love, which contains incalculable prices of infinite value. And besides, when things are done out of pure love, my love finds its outpouring, and it is not insignificant that the creature gives relief and outpouring to the love of the Creator."

November 4, 1914 Volume 11

The new and continuous way to meditate the Passion.

I was doing the Hours of the Passion and Jesus, all pleased, told me: "My daughter, if you knew what great satisfaction I feel in seeing you repeating these Hours of my Passion - always repeating them, over and over again - you would be happy. It is true that my Saints have meditated on my Passion and have comprehended how much I suffered, melting in tears of compassion, so much so, as to feel consumed for love of my pains; but not in such a continuous way, and repeated many times in this order. Therefore I can say that you are the first one to give Me this pleasure, so great and special, as you keep fragmenting within you - hour by hour - my life and what I suffered. And I feel so drawn that, hour by hour, I give you this food and I eat the same food with you, doing what you do together with you. Know, however, that I will reward you abundantly with new light and new graces; and even after your death, each time souls on earth will do these Hours of my Passion, in Heaven I will clothe you with ever new light and glory.

April 23, 1916 Volume 11

At each thought about the Passion of Jesus, the soul draws

light from His Humanity. Continuing in my usual state, my adorable Jesus made Himself seen all surrounded with light, which came out from within His Most Holy Humanity, and embellished Him in such a way as to form an enchanting and enrapturing sight. I remained surprised, and He told me: "My daughter, each pain I suffered, each drop of Blood, each wound, prayer, word, action, step, etc., produced a light within my Humanity, which embellished Me in such a way as to keep all the Blessed enraptured. Now, at each thought that the soul has about my Passion, at each act of compassion, reparation, etc., she does nothing other than draw light from my Humanity, and be embellished in my likeness. So, each additional thought about my Passion will be one more light which will bring her eternal joy."

February 4, 1919 Volume 12

The interior Passion, which the Divinity made the Humanity of Jesus suffer during the course of His whole Life.

Continuing in my usual state, for about three days I felt I was dissolved in God. Many times good Jesus drew Me inside His Most Holy Humanity, and I swam in the immense sea of the Divinity. Oh, how many things one could see! How clearly one could see all that the Divinity operated in His Humanity! Very often my Jesus interrupted my surprises, telling me: "Do you see, my daughter, with what excess of love I loved the creature? My Divinity was too jealous to entrust to the creature the task of Redemption, and so It made Me suffer the Passion. The creature had no power to make Me die as many times for as many creatures which had come, and were to come to the light of Creation, and for as many mortal sins as they would have the disgrace to commit. The Divinity wanted life for each life of creature, and life for each death which she gave herself through mortal sin. Who could be so powerful over Me as to give Me so many deaths, if not my own Divinity? Who would have had the strength, the love, the constancy to watch Me dying so many times, if not my own Divinity? The creature would have grown tired, and would have given up.

And do not think that this crafting of my Divinity started late, but as soon as my Conception was accomplished, even in the womb of my Mama, who many times was aware of my pains, and was martyred, feeling death along with Me. Therefore, even from the maternal womb, my Divinity took on the commitment of loving executioner – but, because loving, more demanding and inflexible; so much so, that not a thorn was spared to my groaning Humanity - not a nail.... But not like the thorns, the nails, the scourges I suffered in the Passion which creatures gave Me, and which did not multiply

-        as many as they inflicted, so many remained. Rather, those of my Divinity multiplied at each offense

-        as many thorns for as many evil thoughts; as many nails for as many unworthy works; as many blows for as many pleasures; as many pains for as many different offenses. They were seas of pains, thorns, nails, and innumerable blows. In the face of the Passion which my Divinity gave Me, the Passion which the creatures gave Me on the last of my days was nothing but the shadow - the image of what my Divinity made Me suffer during the course of my Life. This is why I love souls so much:

they are lives that they cost Me - they are pains inconceivable to created mind. Therefore, enter into my

Divinity, and see and touch with your own hand all that I suffered."

I don't know how - I found myself inside the Divine Immensity, which was raising thrones of Justice for each creature, to which sweet Jesus had to respond for each one of their acts - suffering their pains and death, paying the penalty for everything. And Jesus, like a sweet little lamb, was killed by divine hands, to rise again and to suffer more deaths.... Oh God! Oh God, what harrowing pains! Dying to rise again - and rising again to suffer a yet more excruciating death!

I felt I was dying in seeing my sweet Jesus being killed. Many times I would have wanted to spare just one death for the One who loves me so much. Oh, how well I understood that only the Divinity could make my sweet Jesus suffer so much, and could claim the merit of having loved men to folly and excess, with unheard-of pains and with infinite love. Neither Angel nor man had this power in hand: being able to love us with such heroism of sacrifice - like a God. But who can tell everything? My poor mind was swimming in that immense sea of Light, of Love and of pains; and I remained as though drowned, unable to come out. If my lovable Jesus had not drawn me into the little sea of His Most Holy Humanity, in which the mind is not so submerged - unable to see any boundary, I could have said nothing.

Then, after this, my sweet Jesus added: "Beloved daughter, newborn of my Life, come into my Will - come and see how much there is to substitute for, for my many acts, still suspended, not yet substituted for by creatures. My Will must be within you as the primary gear of a clock: if it moves, all the other gears move, and the clock signals the hours and the minutes. So, all the accord is in the motion of this primary wheel; and if this first wheel has no motion, the clock is stopped. In the same way, the first wheel within you must be my Will, which must give motion to your thoughts, to your heart, to your desires - to everything. And since my Will is the central wheel of my Being, of Creation and of all things, your motion, coming out from that center, will come to substitute for as many acts of creatures. Multiplying in the motions of all as central motion, it will come to place before my Throne, on their behalf, the acts of the creatures, and will substitute for everything. Therefore, be attentive - your mission is great and fully Divine."

March 18, 1919 Volume 12

Pains that Jesus suffered from His Incarnation, having conceived all souls in Himself.

Continuing in my usual state, my always lovable Jesus, making Himself seen, drew me into the immensity of His Most Holy Will, in which He was showing, as though in act, His Conception in the womb of the Celestial Mama. Oh God, what an abyss of love! My sweet Jesus told me: "Daughter of my Will, come to take part in the first deaths and pains that my little Humanity received from my Divinity in the act of my Conception. As I was conceived, I conceived all souls with Me, past, present and future, as my own Life, and I also conceived all the pains and deaths which I had to suffer for each one of them. I had to incorporate everything within Me – souls, pains and deaths, that each one was to suffer, in order to say to the Father: 'My Father, look no longer at the creature, but only at Me. In Me You will find everyone, and I will satisfy

218

for all. As many pains as You want, I will give them to You. Do You want Me to suffer death for each one? I will suffer it. I accept everything, provided You give life to all.' This is why a Divine Power and Will were needed in order to give Me so many deaths and pains, and a Divine Power and Will to make Me suffer. And since in my Will all souls and all things are in act – not in an abstract way, or by intention, as some might think; rather, I kept all of them identified with Me, in reality, and with Me they formed my very Life – in reality, I died for each one, and suffered the pains of all. It is true that it took a miracle of my Omnipotence, the prodigy of my immense Will – without my Will, my Humanity could not have found and embraced all souls, nor could It die so many times.

So, as my little Humanity was conceived, It began to suffer alternating pains and deaths; all souls were swimming in Me as if inside an immense sea, forming the members of my members, the blood of my Blood, the heart of my Heart. How many times did my Mama, taking the first place in my Humanity, feel my pains and my deaths, and She died together with Me! How sweet it was for Me to find the echo of my Love in the love of my Mama! These are profound mysteries, in which the human intellect, not able to understand well, seems to get lost. Therefore, come into my Will, and take part in the deaths and in the pains that I suffered from the moment of my Conception. From this, you will be able to better understand what I tell you."

I am unable to say how, but I found myself in the womb of my Queen Mama, where I could see the tiny little Infant Jesus. But, though tiny, He contained everything. A dart of light flashed from His Heart into mine, and as it penetrated into me, I felt it giving me death; and as it came out, life came back to me. Each touch of that dart produced a most sharp pain, such that I felt undone, and dying, in reality. Then, through the same touch, I felt I was receiving life again. But I don't have the right words to express myself, therefore I stop here.

May 8, 1919 Volume 12

Cause and necessity of the pains that the Divinity gave to the Humanity of Jesus. The reason why He has delayed in making them known.

Finding myself in my usual state, I was thinking of the pains of my adorable Jesus, especially those which His Divinity inflicted upon the Most Holy Humanity of Our Lord. Meanwhile, I felt myself being drawn into the Heart of my Jesus, and I took part in the pains of His Most Holy Heart, which His Divinity made Him suffer during the course of His Life on earth. These pains are very different from those which blessed Jesus suffered in the course His Passion at the hands of the Jews. They are pains which almost cannot be described. From the little I shared in them, I can say that I felt a sharp, bitter pain, accompanied by a rip to the heart itself, such that I felt I was dying in reality; and then Jesus would give me life again with a prodigy of His Love.

Then, after I suffered, my sweet Jesus told me: "Daughter of my pains, know that the pains which the Jews gave Me were the shadow of those which the Divinity gave to Me.

And this was just, in order to receive full satisfaction. In sinning, man offends the Supreme Majesty not only externally, but also internally, and he disfigures in his interior the divine part which was infused in him when he was created. Therefore, sin is formed in the interior of man first, and then comes outside; even more, many times what comes outside is the minimum part, while the greater part remains in his interior. Now, creatures were incapable of penetrating into my interior and of making Me satisfy, by means of pains, the Glory of the Father which they had denied to Him with so many interior offenses. More so, since these offenses wounded the most noble part of the creature – that is, the intellect, the memory and the will - in which the Divine Image is imprinted. Who, then, was to take on this charge if the creature was incapable? Therefore, it was almost necessary that the Divinity Itself take on this commitment, becoming my loving executioner - but more demanding, though loving - in order to receive full satisfaction for all the sins committed in the interior of man.

The Divinity wanted the complete work and the full satisfaction of the creature, both internally and externally. Therefore, in the Passion which the Jews gave to Me I satisfied the external Glory of the Father, which creatures had taken away from Him; in the Passion which my Divinity gave to Me during the course of my whole Life, I satisfied the Father for all the sins of the interior of man. From this you can understand how the pains which I suffered from the hand of the Divinity surpassed by far the pains which creatures gave Me - even more, they almost cannot be compared, and they are less accessible to created mind. Just as there is great difference between the interior and the exterior of man, much greater is the

221

difference between the pains which my Divinity inflicted upon Me and those which creatures gave Me on the last day of my Life. The first ones were cruel, painful, superhuman tearings, capable of giving Me death – and repeated deaths in my most intimate parts, both of the soul and of the body. Not even a fiber was spared Me. The second were bitter pains, but not tearings capable of giving Me death at each pain. But the Divinity had the Power and the Will to do so.

Ah, how much man costs Me! But man, ungrateful, does not care about Me; he does not try to comprehend how much I loved him and how much I suffered for him, to the extent that he has not even come to understand all that I suffered in the Passion which creatures gave Me. And if they do not understand the least, how can they understand the greatest, which I suffered for them? This is why I delay in revealing the innumerable and unheard-of pains which the Divinity gave Me because of them.

But my Love wants to pour Itself out, and to receive love in return. Therefore I call you in the immensity and height of my Will, where all these pains are in act. And not only do you take part in them, but in the name of the entire human family you honor them and give love in return; and together with Me, You substitute for all that creatures owe, but - to my highest pain and great harm to themselves - they don't give it a thought."

June 4, 1919 Volume 12

In order for Redemption to be complete, Jesus was to suffer injustice, hatred, mockeries; and since the Divinity was incapable of giving Him these pains, this is why He suffered the Passion from the hands of creatures on the last of His mortal days.

I was thinking about the Passion of my always lovable Jesus, especially when He found Himself under the storm of the scourges, and I thought to myself: 'When did Jesus suffer more – in the pains which the Divinity made Him suffer during the whole course of His Life, or on the last day from the hands of the Jews?' And my sweet Jesus, with a light which He sent to my intellect, told me: "My daughter, the pains which the Divinity gave Me surpass by far those which creatures gave Me, both in power and in intensity, multiplicity and length of time. However, there was not injustice or hatred, but highest love and accord on the part of all Three Divine Persons in the commitment which I had taken upon Myself to save souls at the cost of suffering as many deaths for as many creatures as would come out to the light of Creation, and which the Father had granted to Me with highest love.

Injustice and hatred do not exist in the Divinity, nor can they exist. Therefore, It was unable to make Me suffer these pains. But man, with sin, had committed highest injustice, hatred, etc., and in order to glorify the Father completely, I was to suffer injustice, hatred, mockeries, etc. This is why, on the last of my mortal days, I suffered the Passion on the part of creatures, in which the injustices, the hatred, the mockeries, the revenges and the humiliations that they used against Me were so many as to render my poor Humanity the opprobrium of all, to the point that I did not look like a man. They disfigured Me so much that they themselves were horrified in looking at Me. I was the abject and the refuse of all. Therefore, I could call them two distinct Passions.

Creatures could not give Me as many deaths or pains, for as many creatures, and as many sins as they would commit. They were incapable of it. Therefore the Divinity took on this commitment, but with highest love and accord on both sides. Besides, the Divinity was incapable of injustice, etc.; so, creatures took over, and I completed the Work of Redemption in everything. How much souls cost Me - this is why I love them so much!"

Another day I was thinking to myself: 'My beloved Jesus has told me so many things; and I - have I been attentive in doing all that He taught me? Oh, how meager I am in pleasing Him! How incapable I feel of everything! So, His many teachings will be my condemnation.' And my sweet Jesus, moving in my interior, told me: "My daughter, why do you afflict yourself? The teachings of your Jesus will never serve to condemn you. Even if you did only once what I have taught you, you would still place a star in the heaven of your soul. In fact, just as I extended a heaven over the human nature and my "Fiat" studded it with stars, in the same way, I extended a heaven in the depth of the soul, and the "Fiat" of the good which she does - because any good is a fruit of my Will - comes to embellish this heaven with stars. Therefore, if she does ten goods, she places ten stars in it; if a thousand, one thousand stars.... So, think rather of repeating my teachings as much as you can, in order to stud the heaven of your soul with stars, so that it will not be inferior to the heaven that shines upon your horizon; and each star will carry the mark of the teaching of your Jesus. How much honor you will give Me!"

August 19, 1922 Volume 14

The pains which the Divinity inflicted on Jesus in His interior. The pains of the Passion were shadows and similes of the interior pains.

As I was in my usual state, sweet Jesus made me suffer part of His pains and of His deaths, which He suffered for each creature. From my little pains I could comprehend how atrocious and mortal the pains of Jesus had been. Then He told me: "My daughter, my pains are incomprehensible to human nature, and the very pains of my Passion were shadows or similes of my interior pains. My interior pains were inflicted on Me by an Omnipotent God, and not one fiber could dodge His blow; those of my Passion were inflicted on Me by men who, having neither Omnipotence nor All-seeingness, were not able to do what they wanted, nor to penetrate into every single fiber of mine.

My interior pains were incarnate, and my very Humanity was transformed into nails, into thorns, into scourges, into wounds, into martyrdom, so cruel as to give Me continuous deaths; and these were inseparable from Me - they formed my very Life. On the other hand, those of my

Passion were extraneous to Me; they were thorns and nails which could be driven inside, and eventually, they could also be removed; and the mere thought that a pain can be removed is a relief. But my interior pains, which were formed of my own flesh - there was no hope that they might be removed, or that the sharpness of a thorn or the piercing of the nails might be lessened.

My interior pains were so great and so many that I could call the pains of my Passion reliefs and kisses given to my interior pains; and uniting together, they gave the last proof of my great and excessive love for the salvation of souls. My external pains were voices which called everyone to enter into the ocean of my interior pains, to make them comprehend how much their salvation cost Me. And then, from your own interior pains, communicated by Me, you can somehow comprehend the continuous intensity of mine. Therefore, pluck up courage - it is love that pushes Me to this."

Printed in Great Britain
by Amazon

43757402R00126